Nobody Home

NOBODY HOME

Writing, Buddhism, and Living in Places

GARY SNYDER

in conversation with
JULIA MARTIN

TRINITY UNIVERSITY PRESS

SAN ANTONIO, TEXAS

Published by Trinity University Press
San Antonio, Texas 78212

Copyright © 2014 by Julia Martin and Gary Snyder

Cover design by Rebecca Lown

Book design by BookMatters, Berkeley, California

Cover art: Gary Snyder, Black Rock Desert, Nevada,
courtesy of the Gary Snyder Archive

Trinity University Press strives to produce its books using methods
and materials in an environmentally sensitive manner. We favor
working with manufacturers that practice sustainable management
of all natural resources, produce paper using recycled stock,
and manage forests with the best possible practices for people,
biodiversity, and sustainability. The press is a member of the
Green Press Initiative, a nonprofit program dedicated to supporting
publishers in their efforts to reduce their impacts on endangered
forests, climate change, and forest-dependent communities.

CIP data on file at the Library of Congress

23   22   21 | 5   4   3

ISBN 978-1-59534-251-5 paperback
ISBN 978-1-59534-252-2 ebook

CONTENTS

South–North, West–East

Crossing the equator
curving over the Atlantic ocean space, south–north, west–east—
Cape Town and Table Mountain, Namaqualand, Kalahari—to Cape
Mendocino, Shasta, Black Rock desert—Julia and I have tossed our
paper airplane letters toward each other now for over thirty years,
mostly swooping ok down

To compare our wild / tame   female / male   scholar / artist
parent / wanderer
tricks with each other. All on the path of walking, writing and sitting.
I've learned so much from her. And I love this neo-Gondwanaland we
share. It's not over yet.

GARY SNYDER

AND FOR THE TIME BEING, THIS BOOK

JULIA MARTIN

One morning in 1984, a letter posted on the other side of the world clacked through the flap of our door in Cape Town. It was from Gary Snyder, a warm response to questions about his writing. I was a graduate student at the time and had been reading his work after a friend gave me a copy of *A Range of Poems*. That first letter was the beginning of a long, long-distance friendship and an ongoing conversation.

It started as an intellectual exchange and became an exploration of practice. As a young person living in a society demarcated by the paranoid logic of apartheid, it was refreshing to meet the spaciousness of Gary's way of seeing. His delight in wildness. Poems that opened up the idea of social justice to include nonhuman beings and the living world. The truly radical realization that things are not *things* but process, nodes in the jeweled net. And in all this a tendency simply to walk out of the narrow prison of dualistic thought.

Over the years, what has kept on bringing me back to Gary's writing and to our conversation is his steady articulation of this vision in practice: Buddhist practice, the practice of writing, of being a householder, of living in places.

This book puts together three interviews and a selection of letters from around thirty years. During this time many things changed decisively—in our personal lives, our local environments, and the world—and these changing conditions are the backstory for an evolving dialogue. When Gary suggested publication and I read it all again (or what I could find), I was filled with a sense of deep gratitude. And of poignant immediacy. Transience. As he describes it in a poem called "One Day in Late Summer":

> This present moment
>   that lives on
>
> to become
>
> long ago

We recorded the first interview, "Coyote-Mind," in 1988 at Kitkitdizze, Gary's home on the San Juan Ridge in the Sierra Nevada. It was a hot day in late August, and Carole Koda, his new partner, sat listening throughout. We talked about writing, about Buddhism, and about community, bioregion, and place. At the time, my take on these was strongly inflected by ideas about gender and the political. After all, where I came from, we were living under a dangerously repressive State of Emergency, and everyone was tuned to ideology. Returning to that dialogue now, I see how often I missed a chance to look deeper because of an attachment to my prepared questions. But Gary responded cheerfully to whatever came up, and the result is quite a far-reaching discussion. Decades later, his position from that time remains prescient and lively. As he put it to me then, in his writing the political involves a "poetic politics" in which "what you launch are challenges and suggestions that don't make sense, or don't begin to add up, for a long, long time."

The next interview took place nineteen years later. Gary had since published some important books, including the masterworks *Practice of the Wild* (1990) and *Mountains and Rivers Without End* (1996). He now spent much of his time at Kitkitdizze looking after Carole, who was ill with cancer. On the other side of the world, I had written a doctoral thesis on environmental literacy and given birth to twins. In the United States, George W. Bush had entered a second term of office in the wake of 9/11, while in South Africa the long dark era of legislated apartheid had ended in 1994 when we all became citizens of a new democracy. As for the state of the earth, the Worldwatch Institute had declared the 1990s the decisive decade for environmental change, but the local-global crisis of environment and development was becoming ever more desperate.

What made this second interview possible was the curious business of international academic conferencing. On my last visit, Gary had given me a heap of papers, among which was the unpublished text of an essay by Cheryll Burgess (later Glotfelty) about something she called "ecocriticism." Within a few years, the Association for the Study of Literature and the Environment (ASLE) was launched, and with it, the beginning of a new critical tendency. By the time Gary and I attended the huge ASLE conference in summer 2005, the organization had become professionalized. He was scheduled to be a keynote speaker and suggested I join him. Do a paper.

This time we sat in his hotel room in Eugene, Oregon, and spoke about suffering and the present moment. Carole was too ill to travel, and the sadness of her absence was palpable. *Danger on Peaks* had appeared the previous year, so far Gary's toughest and most tender response to the suffering of sentient beings. So we talked about its story of the vow he made as a teenager to fight destructive powers, after the bombings of Hiroshima and Nagasaki. He laughed, "I could say, 'Well I tried. And it didn't work, did it? I've been living my life by this and I guess it didn't come to anything. In fact it's worse than ever!'" Then he went on to speak about healing, compassion, and the female Buddha Tara. The conference program was packed, and there were many demands on his time. But within the small space we had, the conversation was open, intimate, and meandering. We called it "The Present Moment Happening."

The third interview, "Enjoy It while You Can," was recorded at Kitkitdizze once again. It was autumn 2010, four years since Carole's death and a few months after Gary's eightieth birthday. He spoke about the experience of "nearing the Exit," and about nondualism and impermanence, while his dog Emi interrupted things occasionally for a lick or a pat. This most recent talk was probably our most serious. It was also the most playful. When I asked about old age, sickness, and death, he said, "Enjoy it while you can! Because soon you won't even have that." As we worked through the transcript afterward, the main question was how to record repeated laughter without making the text repetitive. We decided to leave out all markers. The reader would have to pick it up.

These moments were a rare chance to meet face to face, but most of our dialogue has been in letters and emails, and in the traffic of books, articles, poems, and pictures that has often accompanied them. The early letters tend to explore philosophical and literary questions, but with the passing years, there are more stories.

The main break in the record is 1997–2000. We had recently begun using email and were not well backed up. Inevitably, computers crashed and many letters were lost, but there is one fragment that I've not forgotten. Something about it now seems characteristic of the whole encounter. It was early 1998, and I was wondering about an invitation to participate in Mark Gonnerman's seminar at Stanford on *Mountains and Rivers Without End*. Our twins were about nine months old, and I was still breast-feeding. When I mentioned the idea to Gary he wrote back swiftly that it would be good to see me but added, "I'd sooner risk white-water rafting on the Yukon in flood than attempt international travel with two babies." I would probably have done it anyway, but as it turned out there was no funding.

Reading the letters in sequence now, the urgencies of those years combine to tell a story of journeys, poetry, struggle, children, parents, buddhas, goddesses, work, illness, aging, death, home, play . . . and of the wild regions of Turtle Island and Southern Africa. When I made that first experiment of posting a letter to the United States c/o his publisher, I could never have imagined what a gift this correspondence would become or how much I would learn from Gary's clarity and imagination. His kindness.

And for the time being, this book. What should we call it? The subtitle was easy, a simple description of our main concerns. But the title itself? For its many resonances, I thought of "home." But everything I suggested was too domesticated for a book about Snyder. Then Gary gave it a turn that made new sense. His email said, "I like settling in to the term 'home'—remembering, again, it is the 'oikos' of ecology and economics. And I think of my poem (inspired by a Han-shan poem) that ends 'the mind poet stays in the house / the house is empty and it has no walls / the poem is seen from all sides / everywhere / at once.' Might we try the title as 'Nobody Home'?"

Nobody Home. It had an edge, a spring of surprise. I liked it. Homeless and home. No walls. So here we are at the threshold. I am glad to be sharing these words. The door is open.

INTERVIEWS

COYOTE-MIND

Kitkitdizze • *1988*

JULIA MARTIN: I'd like to start by talking about origins and influences. You've spoken about your childhood before, but what I'm interested in is your experience of growing up in a politically conscious environment: your family was involved in Industrial Workers of the World (IWW) politics. Can you say something about that?

GARY SNYDER: Well, it was a Washington State thirties Depression household, as many households were, in the rural territory just north of Seattle, predominantly settled by Scandinavians with a few Japanese-American households doing truck farming. Our family tradition was radical politics on both sides, particularly on my father's side because my grandfather was an active IWW and socialist speaker and thinker. Then my father was active during the thirties with the League of Unemployed Voters and other left-wing, labor-oriented groups of the time. My mother was sympathetic with those ideas, had essentially the same politics, and was for her time very much a feminist.

The effect of that was for there to be a certain kind of political conversation around the house, certain opinions about the Depression and the economy that I grew up with, a high degree of critical attitude toward some of the more unthinking aspects of the society, and a very critical attitude toward Christianity and the Church. My mother is a militant atheist, my father was a nonmilitant atheist. That, combined with the fact of our poverty and the fact that we worked very hard to keep things going, gave me what you might call a kind of working-class left-wing outlook, from an early age. It involved a certain literary outlook too, because my mother was a student in writing at the University of Washington, and when she was younger she read quite a bit. She wasn't reading during the Depression—I don't think we had any books. So we started going to the public libraries.

MARTIN: Does that background have a significant influence on the way you've constructed your life here at Kitkitdizze, which seems to be a political choice of a kind?

SNYDER: In some sense it certainly feeds into it. Growing up in a rural situation where we kept chickens and cows, cut a little firewood, had an outhouse makes this kind of life very comfortable for me. That is to say, I had many of the skills and attitudes already. I don't think this is an exceptional life, in other words. This is just another way that people live. I like living in the city, and I like living this way too. I don't do it for ideological reasons, or because I think the world is going to come to an end, or civilization is going to collapse and we ought to be self-sufficient.

MARTIN: So you do it because . . . ?

SNYDER: I do it because I like to live this way! I'd live this way even if civilization were going to last. But there is a little difference in attitude that I and my present neighbors bring to it from my father's generation, I think. This generation of back-to-the-land people is very clear on wanting to establish a long-range relationship to a place, and not take it as such an easy thing to move on to another place; to slow down that traditional white-American mobility, which is also rural mobility in many cases, and take the idea of commitment to a place more seriously. So there's a difference in attitude there. That could be said to be somewhat political.

MARTIN: In what respects is this way of living affected by the wider context of capitalist America that you're situated in?

SNYDER: It's affected in absolutely every detail, like everything else is. We live in the same economy, we use the same monetary system, we have to make our living however we can. Being a rural person in America—or anywhere else in the developed world—is in no way to be out of the economy. It's true that there's a small amount of income that comes through what you might call subsistence, through foraging, through gathering, that is nontaxable, which is not counted as income. All of a hunter-gatherer's income is nontaxable, so to speak. So we are to a tiny extent growers and foragers. We could be much more than we are, but it's economically not feasible. There's a higher degree of efficiency to be part of the economy than to opt out of it. In other words, growing food costs you more than buying food at the market. It's a peculiar feature of a more complex economy that there are economic strategies by which you can live in a rural situation without being engaged in rural production. You just happen to do your work in a rural location, rather than an urban location. But there's very little difference from doing your work in a suburb of New York. It's just a matter of where you choose to live.

MARTIN: You are talking about a First World economy, though. Many of the "alternative lifestyles" that are possible here in the United States simply aren't an option where I come from.

SNYDER: I'm sure they are possible where you come from. I'm sure somebody who was skilled in writing and computer programming could live just as well away from town as in town, because of decentralization of the information economy.

MARTIN: But that presupposes a high degree of skill and privilege . . .

SNYDER: I'm sure there are writers in South Africa who don't live right in the middle of downtown, who live out in the country. It requires a little more ingenuity sometimes, but people all over the developed world are doing it—in Scandinavia, England, Wales, Scotland, and many other places. You have to spend more time thinking about tools and maintenance, but it's never accurate to say, "You can do this, but other people can't." I run into that periodically. That is actually not a sensible way of putting it. The fact is, you can if you want to. Anyone can live like this if they're willing to put out the time and the energy. But it's also a matter of what the nature of your work is. There are a lot of people who opt for a lower income to be able to live here. They could make better money if they lived in the city.

MARTIN: Would you say that the way you teach is affected by your attitudes towards authoritarian structures?

SNYDER: I don't think it is. I just teach in as directly communicative a way as I can. I also expect a lot from students. As a teacher I'm authoritarian. . . . You have to be.

MARTIN: That's what a teacher is?

SNYDER: Sure. It's great work—make people get the idea that there are higher standards than what they've been accustomed to, and that improves their sense of what can be done. I think of that as being part of the older milieu, the milieu of student and teacher.

MARTIN: Which models do you have in mind? Where do they come from?

SNYDER: From Buddhist teaching, kiva instruction, from apprenticeship rituals, from my own appreciation of that approach in teachers, and from my understanding of learning. How people learn.

MARTIN: The sort of literature teaching you're doing now must be very different from your own literature training in the fifties, which would have meant New Criticism.

SNYDER: Everything has gone through a lot of changes since then. That was one side of my literary training. The other side was anthropological, where I was exposed to other literary traditions, and to the sense of nonelite cultural features, understanding that all cultures have literature, and that it is not at all necessarily dominated by an elite class: folklore, mythology, folk song.

MARTIN: That position obviously informs your discussion of the Haida myth, "He Who Hunted Bird in His Father's Village," in your BA thesis. Several critics have seen the thesis as a sort of storehouse of ideas and images that have been basic to your later writing. Do you see it like that?

SNYDER: Yes. What I brought together in the thesis were a lot of interests that I'd been exploring. It was a way of trying to synthesize a lot of diverse interests, some of which I'm still exploring. There are other things that are not particularly part of me these days. Obviously, it gave me a good push.

MARTIN: So what stays with you now? Which things are you still exploring?

SNYDER: Well, I'm still interested in the question of the role of myth and nonmyth, the play between direct understanding and perception as against the point of view shaped by cultural structures, direct experience, and any kind of experience mediated by opinion or ideology or preconditions. Unmediated experience—it's an interesting thing. That's what Zen is pointing to: unmediated experience.

MARTIN: So your Zen practice and your interest in anthropology are going in the same direction. On the subject of myth and nonmyth, you wrote at that time that "The function mythology serves in primitive culture is desperately needed in contemporary society." That was the early fifties. Would you still put it like that?

SNYDER: You see, you have to say two things at once. This is the interesting part. We have to say that you need myth. And then you also have to say that you need to get to the end of myth. Myth can be understood as a kind of *provisional* ordering of the situation to get the territory at least clear enough so you can begin to work on it. In a so-called primitive culture, myth works to give a shape and a wholeness to a wide range of behaviors and institutions. Sometimes it's extraordinarily shapely and very well constructed in some way: one symbol informs another symbol, and such a society has tremendous strength. However, the way mythologies work is by no means always benign. And so we have another way of speaking about myth, which is to speak of it as superstition, prejudice, preconceptions, blinders on the eyes, blinders on the mind, views and opinions that trap people. So mythology, images, can be used in more ways than one. We need to be able to discriminate between visions that liberate and visions that enslave, myths that liberate and myths that do not.

MARTIN: In your thesis you emphasized the mytheme of the supernatural wife and stressed the idea of "Woman" as mythic image of "the totality which can be known." Can you comment on what this view of a mythic Woman has involved in your work?

SNYDER: Yes, there are a number of feminine images that overlap in there. The phenomenal world as female, as illusion, is one.

MARTIN: Maya.

SNYDER: Yes. The phenomenal world as totality of that which may be known, as a *magna mater*, or a goddess of nature, is another. The two are one and the same, though. The phenomenal world is either illusion or it's not illusion, depending on how you look at it. Either way, it is given in some traditions a feminine imagery.

Those are images, I'm quite sure, that are projected by men. The phenomenal world, as both what can be known and what cannot be known, can be seen in a *nongendered* way as the Tao. In Vajrayana and Hindu symbolic meta-physics they actually switch the genders back and forth, and in Hinduism the masculine is seen as the quies-cent and the feminine as the active. In some schools of Buddhism, the universe as illusion is seen as the feminine and the universe as insight or wisdom is seen as the mas-culine, and sometimes that's switched. The more you get into it, the less important the gender imagery becomes. In Zen, the terminology is "host and guest"—it doesn't matter which gender you're talking about. You're talking about the interplay of the apparently dichotomous nature of the universe and the fact that it's actually not dichot-omous. It's one. And yet it plays back and forth between emptiness and phenomena, in time and out of time, the karmic fabric and the essential position, without time.

So I'm not as much interested in the *genderization* of

those things. But I see the *use* of gender imagery in India in its poetic mythology and Tibet in its poetic mythology as charming—and sometimes useful. You might say that in a bhakti tradition, they tend to concretize their imagery into gender and have goddesses and gods. And in a gnostic tradition, a jnana tradition, a wisdom tradition, they would prefer not to see it as a gender-tied imagery.

MARTIN: In terms of your own work, would you see yourself as making use of both traditions, bhakti and jnana? There's a lot of goddess mythology in your poems.

SNYDER: Certainly.

MARTIN: I'm thinking particularly of the goddess Gaia. When you write about Gaia, it seems to indicate some sort of identification with those ecofeminists and deep ecologists who have been using the term in the last decade or so.

SNYDER: I took Gaia from the beginning as a very useful, charming way of giving a word to the biosphere. Gaia is not all of the phenomenal universe, nor does it refer to an illusory realm. It refers to something very limited and very specific: the biosphere on Planet Earth. So it's not talking about matter or nature, but about one particular organism and its history.

MARTIN: Is the use of a goddess as image for the biosphere a strategic choice, a counter to patriarchal mythologies?

SNYDER: It's historical. Because the *ge* is what we have for *geology*. I wouldn't support it for too long, because you get into trouble as soon as you ask. "Now what's the opposite of Gaia?" or "What's the male of Gaia?"

MARTIN: And then?

SNYDER: Solar energy? Okay . . . now solar energy is coming in and doing all this stuff with chemicals and making life. That's okay, but you don't want to pursue those images very long. It gets too literal. So I take it as a nonliteral image, and I wrote a few poems called "Songs for Gaia," more interested in developing the scale of the image than anything literal. You know, "How large an organism can you imagine?" But I really get bored with all these New Age types that go around holding Gaia conferences all the time now, as though they were talking about something real.

MARTIN: You would see the term as a provisional myth, in other words.

SNYDER: Yes. And also it's an interesting scientific fact, or possibly scientific fact.

MARTIN: That's Lovelock's Gaia Hypothesis.

SNYDER: Yes. Better that people should not get too carried away with talking about archetypes and stuff when they're talking about Gaia, and should stay with the interesting question of "How large an organism is life?"

and "How does an organism of that scale work if it works? What is the chemistry of it?" That's much more interesting. Too many of these people want to jump over the details of biology right back into mythology before they've got themselves grounded in it. So I backed off from the use of the term Gaia, except as an interesting metaphor. I presume the hypothesis to have some use as a hypothesis. But talking about the planet as Gaia per se will not do the planet a lot of good. You still have to find a course of action, a program. Do something active: "Where do we go from here?"

MARTIN: What about the more general connection of "woman" and "nature"?

SNYDER: That's a good question. Carolyn Merchant (who wrote *The Death of Nature*) and I were talking about that. There are definitely two schools of feminist thought about it. Ynestra King, for example, wants to eliminate all gendered references to nature. She says that doesn't help women. It just makes them look fecund and Great Mothery, and it keeps them in the kitchen. Then there's another imagery that is certainly very deeply established in thought and lore: metaphors drawn from some obvious observations of seeds being planted and sprouting, birth processes in nature, which suggest an analogy with women's bodies and their roles in culture. I don't know if hunter-gathering people ever got so deeply fertility- and goddess-oriented as did agrarian people. In agriculture there is the very clear metaphor of scratching the ground, poking a hole, and then dropping a seed in it, covering it up and watching it sprout. It becomes very easy to see the sun and the sky as some kind of fertilizing forces, and the earth as a womb which holds the seed and then brings it out. Hunter-gathering people do not genderize nature in the way that early agrarian cultures do.

MARTIN: How useful can that sort of early agrarian metaphor be for the late-twentieth-century people?

SNYDER: Well, you can take "woman" to mean "generative force," assigning more of the reproductive role to the female than the male, which is the way that some people might see it. (There is some biological truth in this. In some animals the female has a more nurturing capacity than the male.) And *then* you can continue the image and say "our mother Earth," and say "We shouldn't destroy our mother Earth." So it becomes ecological language. To be more precise, "We shouldn't destroy our mother Earth and our father—whatever the father is." If there are forces at work, and there are two of them, we need both of them. So . . . I'm just playing with these things still myself. We should respect the wholeness of the enterprise, the familiarity, the complementarity of the whole organic process.

MARTIN: You referred to two trends in feminist thought about the metaphoric association of "woman" and "nature." Would you agree that it is precisely *that* association that has legitimized the oppression of women?

SNYDER: Clearly, in some cases.

MARTIN: You also spoke of a "male projection."

SNYDER: For some of it . . .

MARTIN: I'm interested in the differences between the way, say, radical feminists might write about "woman and nature," and their responses to the use of similar terminology by male writers. Someone like Adrienne Rich has been very critical of the celebration by male writers of what they might call "the feminine." Any comments? To what extent is your use of such terminology conditioned by your gender?

SNYDER: Well, I'm sure it is. I think it's tedious to get too involved in trying to figure out those arguments. I mean, everyone has an agenda.

MARTIN: As well as a gender. . . . Would you call yourself a feminist?

SNYDER: I don't think it would be appropriate for a man to call himself a feminist. There are many women who wouldn't call themselves feminists. So it's a role that's appropriate for women, and I support feminists, although I don't support all feminists. I don't support feminists who are just out there to buy into the capitalist system and become managers. That seems like a very revisionary form of feminism. I don't necessarily support a feminism of women's uniqueness, either. I *do* feel that the force of feminism in, for example, Japanese culture is very important, is in some ways truly revolutionary, and is more unsettling to the culture than industrialization and modernization have been.

MARTIN: What about the questions feminism raises for Zen Buddhism, which has traditionally been very much a male line?

SNYDER: Zen teaching seems to be able to incorporate women easily, as in a lot of places in the States. What's interesting is to hear what Zen women who practice Buddhism have to say, their views toward Buddhist practice and toward feminism. There are some women who will say (having come from a feminist background) that they came to Buddhism because they needed a study of who they really were, without preconceptions, without a feminist or an antifeminist agenda. To ask yourself "What is my nature really like?" without the presumption that it's going to be particularly female or male: to go beyond the gender side of the question and just look at what it is, to observe what your mind and psyche does. So they found Buddhism very refreshing in its freedom from preconceptions about the way the mind is. Buddhism teaches that the mind is the mind, and that the difference between a woman's mind and a man's mind at deeper levels is absolutely zero. So when Buddhism is doing what it should be doing, it helps us all equally, before race or gender, in establishing an insight into our own nature. And it may be that that insight includes some understanding of this part of me, this component which you might call feminine. That calls for some acknowledgment, and I need not be afraid of it or ashamed of it. And the same for men too—there has to be a place where they can acknowledge what part of their makeup is generated by their gender.

MARTIN: By their socialization *into* that gender?

SNYDER: *Prior* to socialization. Well, socialization into gender, but also, you know, there are forces at work that are prior to socialization. You see it in the difference between different girls and different boys. Some girls will be frilly and feminine from the very beginning. Some won't. And I see it around here, we all see it: we've seen mothers who are handling chain saws and driving trucks, whose daughters won't touch them. They simply won't do that. There is a character that you're born with, and there are tendencies that are prior to what your parents have socialized you into. There are definitely tendencies among girls to do certain things in certain ways, and there are tendencies in boys to do certain things, *prior* to socialization. *Then* socialization can enforce certain things or play down certain things. But you're not dealing with a totally blank slate.

MARTIN: With regard to gender, Buddhism would seem then to reject the idea that differences such as "male" and "female" indicate fixed essences, fixed givens.

SNYDER: Buddhism would say that the male / female differences are real enough, but on a fairly illusory level, and that our essential nature is free of that. After all, our essential nature is the nature of rocks and trees, and there are no men and women there. So gender has very little to do with the essential insight, and in koan study, and the primary awakening called satori, or with the subsequent insights that people have. The way women grasp koans and the way men grasp koans is absolutely the same— there's no difference at all. There's no gender difference. There are some sides of Buddhist mythology that do put women down, it's true. And in some traditions those lines may be quoted from time to time, and in other traditions they won't. Zen has *always* held that there's no difference between men and women with respect to practice.

MARTIN: But historically, that's not how monasteries have been run.

SNYDER: No, because the *society* has not supported that. The

Buddhists say that women and men are equal in their capacity for achieving enlightenment. But the society is not sending them equal numbers of men and women—for other reasons, for reasons that are already established in the society at large.

MARTIN: As I understand it, the version of Buddhist practice that you're developing at the Ring of Bone Zendo emphasizes *this* place, *this* experience. You don't want it to be an Asian import.

SNYDER: Yes, North American. The other thing we're trying to do is to keep ourselves, so to speak, local. In that sense we're more orthodox, more Asian, than many of the Zen centers that have been established, in the usual modern mode of establishing a center that caters to rootless and alienated people that come and go, and bring their problems, who are sampling the smorgasbord of therapies and possibilities for themselves in modern urban life. Most Zen centers draw on the alienated, educated members of the upper middle class. They also tend to carry on traditional Japanese Buddhist forms without any critical thought. That is the way that new cults worked in Rome.

MARTIN: In Rome?

SNYDER: That's the way that new religions functioned in Rome in the second and third century AD, as symptomatic of the breakdown of the fabric of society; contending alien cults in a collapsing society. That's not a very interesting place to be. What's more interesting to me is something that is quite a bit deeper. First of all, what happens when you begin to have something a little more like a real community, and you can look at the possibilities of a sort of "postrevolutionary socialism," or what Paul Goodman calls "a natural society."

MARTIN: What does that mean in particular? Can you give some examples?

SNYDER: It means a society in which people live in one place for a good number of years; it means that they know each other personally on a first-name basis; it means that they know a *considerable* amount of the personal history of the individuals concerned; it means that they know their own family history and that they keep in touch with their parents; it means that they are engaged in their community in one or another ways by serving on committees, formal and informal committees; it means that they do not expect everybody to do what they do—a community in its own nature cannot be homogenous.

MARTIN: As would be the case in an intentional community.

SNYDER: We're talking about a *natural* community.

MARTIN: And you'd see an intentional community as being artificial.

SNYDER: An intentional community can enforce a point of

view. A natural community is a *culture*. Consequently, points of view are formed almost subliminally, over the long run, by the totality of the experiences that people go through and by the songs and the stories that they tell each other. So on many levels such a place is, so to speak, self-motivating. So that's a natural community, a symptom of a natural society.

I don't think Buddhism can function in a way that's truly beautiful, truly interesting, until it has a natural society as its ground. *Then* the truly existential problems become the problems you're dealing with. You get the politics out of the way by having a sane society. Then you can begin to work on the really *refined* study of the mind. This is what I've understood from working in Asia, that *that* is what Buddhism was doing at its best. We are in an era of tremendous social and political breakdown. Buddhism is not the cure for that, although it may be of help. But it can only be *one* of the kinds of measures.

So that's why I divide my time between what you may call culture-building, or community-building, and Buddhist teaching. It would be really easy to live in the city and teach at a Zen center and do nothing but Buddhist teaching. I wouldn't want to do it that way. I'd rather go out and start working in the neighborhoods as much as I could because I think you have to work the ground for a

Buddhist society first. You can't just leave your society the way it is and say "We offer this as one of the teachings." You've got to help the society get its feet on the ground before those teachings can begin to flourish.

MARTIN: You've talked about "getting politics out of the way," and yet that seems to be premised on an idea of radical social transformation, at the local level at least. You also used the term "postrevolutionary." Would you call yourself a revolutionary?

SNYDER: I'd call myself a postrevolutionary! I guess I'd call myself a revolutionary in the sense that I can clearly envision situations, actually practical social structures, that are well beyond and *after* the kinds of conditions that people are living under now. And I can recognize that those possibilities are real, not impractical, not utopian. But it will take some drastic changes before we can get there. I'm not sure that deliberately applied drastic changes will necessarily get you where you want to go. So I'm a little bit cautious about proposing programs. There are a few things I propose.

MARTIN: Such as?

SNYDER: Don't move. That's very revolutionary. That's why it catches people by surprise. They can't figure out why it's revolutionary for a long time. It takes a while to start seeing that it is.

MARTIN: I suppose my questions make it clear that I see your work as often being explicitly ideological, political. Would you agree?

SNYDER: I imagine that my work is political in the sense of its engagement in issues of import regarding the manner of the directions of our societies and issues of import in the manner of fundamental ethical attitudes. *That's* where it is political, like Blake was political. And I don't expect some of the things that I propose poetically, so to speak, to make sense, maybe, for decades. So that's poetic politics, where what you launch are challenges and suggestions that don't make sense or don't begin to add up for a long, long time.

Politics is also just drama. I know people who do politics as their art form, who are actually very clear about that: "I could write poetry, I could be a painter. I like to do street theater, I like to do politics as theater. This is my theater." There are a lot of people who do that. So it's not interesting, really, to separate art and politics: politics is a kind of theater in which the stage is your own society, as you go back and forth on it. So ecological politics is mountains-and-fields theater. It's a large-scale theater of the surface of the planet. Gaia is a theatrical device. The mother goddess is another mask of theater.

MARTIN: To be used for as long as it serves its purpose?

SNYDER: Yes, as long as it plays. And how it plays, and what happens when it plays, is fun to watch. And the stakes are real. The stakes *are* real. The stakes have to do with a kind of sustained viability in its diversity, without utopian or perfectionistic expectations. It would just be nice if we could keep going.

MARTIN: You made a comment in *Turtle Island* that has stuck with me as a puzzle: "Knowing that nothing need be done, is where we begin to move from." What did you mean, exactly?

SNYDER: Yes, that's a Buddhist point. Lots of people have asked me about that. In the larger scale, things *will* take care of themselves. It's obviously human hubris to think we can destroy the planet, can destroy life. It's just another exaggeration of ourselves. Actually we can't. We're far too small.

MARTIN: *Really?*

SNYDER: The time scale is far too large, and the resistance of cellular life is far too great. Lovelock is very interesting on this, on the extraordinary resilience of cells. But that's no excuse. That would be no excuse for doing things poorly. A kind of bottom line is that all human activity is as trivial as anything else. We can humbly acknowledge that and excuse ourselves from exaggerating our importance, even as a threat, and also recognize the scale and the beauty of things. And *then* go to work. Don't imagine that we're doing ecological politics to save the world. We're doing ecological politics to save ourselves, to save our souls. It's a *personal* exercise in character and in manners. It's a matter of etiquette. It's a matter of living right. It's not that the planet requires us to be good to it. It's that we must do it because it's an aesthetic and ethical choice.

MARTIN: Would you say, then, that there's a lot of hysteria out there? What about the ozone hole?

SNYDER: Those issues are all real. Those issues are all real, but they're not total. And the power of the universe far surpasses any damage we can do to it.

MARTIN: One response to the ecological crisis that you have been associated with is the deep ecology movement, or what you have referred to as "depth ecology." Can you say something about this?

SNYDER: "Deep ecology" is not my term, it's Arne Naess's term. It just means, to my notion, people who are serious about ecology and aware of the larger-scale importance of the whole array of creatures and processes in the biosphere and don't rate human beings as being necessarily the most interesting or the most important part of that. So that's where they are: nonanthropocentric, and they call it biological egalitarianism. I don't think that there is any shame in being a human being, and being pro-human. I think we should take that as being part of the turf. We're not *forced* to practice human guilt, feel guilty about being a human being, any more than you need to have any other guilt about who you are. But still they have a lot of good points to make: that rough distinction of resource management ecology as shallow and long-term, life-respecting strategies for the benefit of all as deep ecology is important.

"Depth ecology" is a term that I'm working with now. I developed it when I started trying to do an ecological and etymological myth analysis of the widely distributed sub-Arctic study of the girl who married a bear. My method of analysis of that story came out of what I would call depth ecology, which is going to be in my book [*The Practice of the Wild*]. The term would refer to a territory where myth or folklore or shamanic constructions have to do with the way you treat creatures, whether or not you kill them or don't kill them. How do you kill a bear? What do you do with a bear when you've killed it? Who eats it, who doesn't eat it? What part of the bear do women and children eat, what part of the bear do old men eat? That's . . . depth ecology.

MARTIN: So your understanding of ecological work is something very different from environmentalism.

SNYDER: One would do environmentalist work in the sense

of dealing with little issues as they came up—we all do that—whereas the ecological view is a larger-scale view, one that is more biological. You can be an environmentalist without knowing anything about biology, just as you can be a politician without any knowledge of anthropology.

MARTIN: I'm thinking particularly of Murray Bookchin's critique of what he calls "mere environmentalism."

SNYDER: Yes, I know pretty much what Murray would say. Part of it is just exercises in terminologies. I don't put people down for working on issues, especially if they win something. Whether or not they understand the larger picture, we have to be grateful for people who get out there and save a marsh. The same would be true of any political affairs. So what's the use of putting them down? They're working within their abilities . . . and that's wonderful.

MARTIN: You mentioned earlier that your upbringing led you to be critical towards Christianity, and you've often written about the connection you see between Western metaphysics and the current ecological crisis. Can you see any ways that the work you're involved in, in Buddhism particularly, might benefit from Christian or Occidental religious traditions?

SNYDER: That's an interesting question. Of course Western Buddhists, coming out of Western culture and being probably from Christian or Jewish backgrounds, are already bringing those things into Buddhism, by virtue of their personalities and their background. So there's already some kind of exchange there, I'm sure.

My own view is that Buddhism can profit from, but wouldn't necessarily want to emulate, an understanding of the Christian concern for history—and the historical fact of the Christian concern for personality—as a kind of leavening factor in the evolution of Buddhist thought. I think that the Buddhists also have to admire the commitment of certain Christian sects, such as Quakers, to *peace*, and the Christian idea of witness and bearing witness as a matter of conscience. It has pitfalls from a Buddhist standpoint, pitfalls of over ego-stimulation. But that side of Christian engagement is admirable. It certainly can be learned from. Buddhists can learn from, or at least take note of, the section of the Church that is doing liberation theology. Buddhism has been quiescent, socially, for much of its history, and what and how it becomes more active in the social sphere is going to be very interesting. I'm sure it will, because in the West everybody gets more social. And also the power makes a difference: political action, political involvement, makes a difference in a pluralistic democracy, whereas in a traditional Asian culture, there's very little direct political action possible.

MARTIN: Would you see your work as a counter to that traditional quiescence?

SNYDER: Yes, well what I see is . . . an interesting vision proposed by Mahayana Buddhism that hasn't been acted out much, hasn't been actualized much. I think that it may be the destiny for Western Buddhists to try to make the effort of *actualizing* what Buddhists say they can do in terms of actual life in society.

MARTIN: Can you be more specific?

SNYDER: Part of the actualization of Buddhist ethics is, in a sense, to be a deep ecologist. The actualization of Buddhist insights gives us a Buddhist economics not based on greed but on need, an ethic of adequacy but simplicity, a valuation of personal insight and personal experience over possessions. What I like most about Buddhism really is its fearlessness. So much of what warps people is fear of death and fear of impermanence. So much of what we do is simply strategies to try and hold back death, trying to buy time with material things. So at its best Buddhism provides people with a way of seeing their own frailty: you need less in the way of material objects and fortresses around yourself.

MARTIN: I'd like to talk about what you meant in *Turtle Island* by the phrase "bringing a voice from the Wilderness, my constituency." What does this say about your role as Buddhist, ecologist, poet? You've written elsewhere about cor-respondences between "wilderness" and "the unconscious."

SNYDER: I think I'd just like to leave that because as an image it generates enough as it is. It's something that is quite adequate, once suggested.

MARTIN: It finds its own way? Okay. Perhaps we can just talk about "voice." In *Regarding Wave,* the central metaphors, as I see it, derive from images associated with the god-dess Vak, or Voice. Is the concept of Vak as "the voice of Dharma" still useful to you now?

SNYDER: Vak is just another way of referring to speech. I haven't done anything further with Sanskrit language theory or mantra theory. In Buddhism, though, they say the sense of hearing, the vehicle of sound, is the clearest and easiest and most appropriate vehicle for enlighten-ment. We proceed to learn from the sense of sound better than from any other sense, in the very specific terms of Zen enlightenment. So that's why Kuan Yin's name means "observe the sounds." That's very clearly stated in Vajrayana mythology. It also says that the present *kalpa* is presided over by Amitabha, whose color is red and who resides in the West. Amitabha's active compassion emanation in the material universe is Avalokiteshvara, "observe the sound, learn by hearing." And that's exactly what happens: sound is essentially your path in.

It's a different point, although it's related, that literature and poetry are fundamentally oral, because language is oral, and writing is secondary. I understand that some French intelligentsia don't believe that, but they really have it backwards. In fact, one of Derrida's biggest weaknesses is his insistence on theorizing from written texts. A whole lot of what he's trying to say falls apart if you go back to orality. There's a Jesuit teacher who's written on this. . . .

MARTIN: Walter Ong, *Orality and Literacy*? He does mention deconstruction near the end.

SNYDER: Yes, that's it.

MARTIN: Sound is the way in. But then, if, as Taoism at least proposes, "The Way which can be spoken is not the Way," how (or why) write poems (or even sing them)? Can you say something about what seems to be the paradox of composing a Zen poem: how to give expression to an experience that is presymbolic, preverbal?

SNYDER: What you quoted was the first line of the first chapter of the *Tao te Ching*, which is often translated as "The Way that can be spoken of is not the true Way." That may not be the only translation. The translation I prefer treats the second "Tao" as a verb, and would translate as "The Way that can be *followed* is not the true or correct Way," which puts a different twist to it. Anyway, I don't think it's correct that "that which can be said" is automatically not true. To the contrary, in Zen we find that that which *cannot* be said is not complete. If you have an understanding and cannot express it, then your understanding is not yet complete. The act of expressing clarifies your understanding of it. However, the nature of that expression may not be clear and transparent to everybody, which is why Zen literature is not easy to follow. But that's what it is. So the person who has a Zen eye can understand it.

I think in general it's dangerous to propose . . . there's been a lot of mischief that has proceeded from the idea that the truth cannot be said. It gets people off the hook too easily.

MARTIN: Inscrutable silences?

SNYDER: Exactly. A Zen teacher won't accept that, absolutely won't accept it. You go before a Zen teacher and he says, "Well, what is *mu*? What is the nondual essence of the mind?" And you just sit there and smile beatifically. He'll say, "Come on, get off it."

MARTIN: How does this idea of "the Way that can be followed" relate to what you said earlier about teachers, the value of an authoritarian teaching tradition?

SNYDER: Well, you have to learn how to go on a way before you quit following it.

MARTIN: Charles Olson wrote in the sixties about the need

for poetry to get rid of "the lyrical interference of the ego, of the subject and his soul." Would this describe what you're attempting to do?

SNYDER: Yes, I'm not interested in being a consistent poet speaking voice, speaking for my own sentiments and sensibilities.

MARTIN: Because?

SNYDER: Because it's not interesting. It's like talking about yourself.

MARTIN: And what is interesting?

SNYDER: Talking about your nonself! When a bird flies across from one tree to another tree, you can be the bird flying across from one tree to another tree. You don't have to *think* about the bird, how you feel about the bird. No difference between self and universe. So just shortcut that illusion.

MARTIN: But "self" informs the way you read the bird.

SNYDER: But you don't have to encourage it. Which isn't to say that sometimes poems aren't written in the first person. The point is not to let yourself be the main character of what you're thinking. If the sense of self is too narrowly located, then people sound like they're talking about themselves all the time.

MARTIN: Do you evolve conscious strategies other than your formal Zen practice for developing this sort of attitude?

SNYDER: Zen practice is not limited to sitting on a cushion in a zendo. That becomes a habit of life, that's true.

MARTIN: In the poem "What Have I Learned" you describe a lifetime's knowledge of how to use certain "tools." It's clear that the term means many things in this context. "What have I learned / but the proper use for several tools . . . " Can you say more about this?

SNYDER: I was thinking of such tools as language, the library . . .

MARTIN: Your word processor?

SNYDER: No, more general: the whole fact of the stored body of information that is accessible to us at any time—you go up to the library—which means all the referencing and information research skills.

MARTIN: The poem refers to "passing it on." Is that what you see yourself passing on?

SNYDER: Not exactly. What one hopes to pass along is the living experience of being in each moment.

MARTIN: You've spoken about the oral roots of literature and Vak as speech. How important is oral performance for your poetry?

SNYDER: I enjoy reading my own and others' poems aloud. If somebody other than myself did it, that would be okay. I feel that the primary mode of existence of poetry is in speech and performance, and that writing is a secondary mode of existence. That's where it's been put *down*, where it's been kept. Just like a play: you know when you read a play that its full mode of existence would be in performance. Still, you know that you can get something out of it by reading the script. So a poem is a kind of script—at least it can sometimes be that way; I think of a poem in that way. By thinking that way and by practicing that way I do make a connection in my own poetics with a very broad tradition of poems, the preliterate and oral traditions.

MARTIN: To what extent does the sort of poetics you have in mind imply a rejection of the dominant Western literary tradition?

SNYDER: It doesn't reject the *poems*. There's some excellent poetry there. It rejects the limitations that it has imposed on us: the elitist limitations, transforming itself into an academic discipline, where its works are kept in libraries.

MARTIN: Do you have any suggestions for people who are working in a primarily literate culture and want to access oral tradition so as to incorporate some of its features in their own poetry?

SNYDER: That is something that we've been just making up as we went along, and there's been a lot of exchange back and forth between people in drama, storytellers, and some traditional Native people, and the artists who've been doing it. It's very lively now. Performance poetry is being done all the time in New York, Los Angeles, and San Francisco. You go to a lot of theater and performance and get a sense of what's happening, of what can be done. You try things out. Try things out in your living room.

MARTIN: More specifically, do you have any advice for writers who are experimenting with forms that don't reproduce the old relation between reader and writer?

SNYDER: We did an event at Green Gulch Farm, a branch of San Francisco Zen Center, a year ago last April, where we had a poetry creation right in the zendo, with a great deal of randomness and unpredictability, à la John Cage. It's fun, but it's not memorable. The writer-reader is the singer-hearer relationship. Traditionally, you break down the line between the singer and the hearers with responses or choruses where people join in the chorus, sing together. There's a play that goes back and forth between the singer and the hearers, with the singer or singers who occupy the central territory invading the territory of the audience, including the audience in their territory, and then backing out again. I have no problem with that, I have no problem with the singer-hearer, reader-writer relationship. It's a voluntary association. Nobody is forced to be a reader or a hearer, and so I would not call it a model of oppression. You can walk out if you want to. In fact, it has a good free-market analogy. It's the market: pay and enjoy, or don't buy. You go down the alleys and lanes of a fair, and you go in to find which jugglers you want to see. The writer or the artist has no complaint. People either come to hear their wares or they don't.

MARTIN: With the free-market analogy in mind, how would you respond to the criticism that your work tends to be too esoteric, too dependent on allusions that most readers will not get?

SNYDER: Some does, some doesn't. Some of my writing is more esoteric, some is less. I try to put in something for everybody.

MARTIN: And who is your audience?

SNYDER: The primary audience is people born since 1925, living in California, Oregon, Washington, British Columbia, and Alaska.

MARTIN: That's pretty regional.

SNYDER: That's primary. That's where people live who can get a sense of what the inside levels are. People can read it in other places, but they'll miss some.

MARTIN: Why that date?

SNYDER: Because that's when the zeitgeist becomes . . . the zeitgeist of this particular *zeit* . . . that's this *zeit*, this time frame.

MARTIN: I was recently reading the poem "Front Lines" with

some of my students in South Africa, most of whom were born in the late sixties. I told them I was going to be seeing you, and asked if I should pass on any questions. So after a highly charged account of ecosocial exploitation, the poem ends with the words, "And here we must draw / our line." The students' response was "That's fine. But if we accept your critique, what do we do?"

SNYDER: Well the bioregional program is very good. That is the one that says "First, don't move, and second, find out what that teaches you." It means you have to learn local history, local economics; not just in the abstract, but as it affects you locally. You're asking, "How are we related to the economy exactly, detail by detail?" I know exactly how much gravel is worth. I know how the price of timber has fluctuated over the last fifteen years. There are a lot of instructive things you learn about how you're related to the economy. I can't know what South African students are faced with, but if they feel they have a right to be where they are at all, then they should be there and they should take it on as a serious obligation. They should think up where they want to raise their children, and then they should provide a place for their children. That doesn't necessarily mean in the country.

A few things, then: one is a place, one is your mind. That means meditation in one form or another, as a nonstressful, nonhysterical lifetime process, just a habit of life. A third thing is to have a craft, have a skill, have *one thing* that you can do. If it's something you can do with your hands, all the better. Have a *real* skill, for the sake of yourself, and for the sake of others. Those are very fundamental. I would say that political sanity and engagement can in part come out of a curriculum like that. Not 100 percent. If a person as a matter of career has chosen the life of a political warrior, then that involves some other kinds of action.

MARTIN: We were speaking this morning before the interview about pressure on writers to conform to ideological positions that are considered to be "politically correct." Would you mind repeating what you said?

SNYDER: It seems to me, by my (by no means thoroughly researched) historical information, that putting a high degree of importance on the fine points of doctrine, and on the idea of the correct line, the correct doctrine, comes into Occidental culture in a big way with the Catholic Church and its various councils in which it declared certain positions heretical or false. The importance that they placed on that and the inability to accept these poetically different versions, or different aspects of the same truth, and the continual seeking-out, arguing-out of doctrinal points has dominated much of Christian thought. This means that the possession of, or the adherence to, a correct line now seems to take precedence over action or meditation or prayer, in a big way. I see it continuing right into the old Communist Party's paranoid obsession with the correct line, and you know radical movements today for which there can be no diversity regarding the line. It's what is going on right now with the feminists and deep ecologists and Murray Bookchin, all arguing about what's the vanguard and what's the right line. Murray Bookchin's main complaint is that he's not the vanguard. He wants to be the vanguard and he's mad because Earth First! is the vanguard, and so he has to criticize Earth First! all the time. That is elevating the theory over the practice, and it need not be done that way. There are other ways to accomplish clarification of doctrine without being so intellectual or abstract about it. The whole thing is an Occidental neurosis.

MARTIN: At the same time, there is surely a place for vigilance. Having grown up in South Africa, I'm aware of the possibilities for unwittingly internalizing the dominant ideology while attempting to articulate something that is an alternative to it, which is outside it. Are you conscious of that in your work? Do you deliberately work against it?

SNYDER: Yes, I certainly try to watch out for it. It's a danger on the Buddhist level—I mean, that really is on the level of understanding what it is that's affecting you, understanding how you are shaped, understanding what the deeper levels of your opinions and thoughts and feelings are. Those things are so unconscious. You also have to find out what the dominant ideology is, and how it changes. That's tricky. It isn't just that you set yourself against it, because if you set yourself too totally against it, you can't talk to it. If you don't understand how indoctrinated you are, then there's no communication possible. That takes a certain coyote-mind.

MARTIN: Trickster?

SNYDER: Yes, coyote-mind can understand both sides of a question anytime. *Really* understand them.

MARTIN: Is that a way of approaching Zen's nondualism?

SNYDER: Yes.

MARTIN: And how would these questions relate to the problems of a program focused on celebrating "woman as nature"?

SNYDER: Okay. Let's see how a program celebrating woman as nature is unwittingly buying into the dominant ideology. For one thing, it might involve organizing a group of people to be an audience to celebrate something that is given an authority above them. Structurally it's no different from celebrating the flag. So instead of looking to content you look at form, and form is the form of masses elevating authority. That's acting with the dominant ideology.

MARTIN: And yet you've written poems that could be described as celebrating woman as nature?

SNYDER: Oh, I might have done that once or twice, as an exercise, and as I felt like it. But I can also look back and say, "Well, maybe I was just reproducing . . . the Fourth of July or something," reproducing a form that is more insidious than one might have thought. Those are interesting questions.

THE PRESENT
MOMENT HAPPENING

Eugene, Oregon • 2005

JULIA MARTIN: Gary, in *Danger on Peaks* there is clearly so much awareness of suffering and destruction at many levels, yet the collection is also deeply concerned with healing. So the main question that comes to mind for me when reading the poems is once again about how to work with integrity as a writer in the late modern world. At the same time I've also been wondering how this collection's particular response to the experience of suffering and healing might relate to your understanding of the female Buddha Tārā—who appears quite significantly in some of the earlier work. In *Mountains and Rivers Without End*, for example, you have described that whole epic poem as a sort of sutra for Tārā. Now, although she isn't mentioned explicitly, there seem to be some continuities in what you're doing.

Let's approach these questions through the poems. I'd like to start by talking about the vow that you made as a fifteen-year-old and now return to near the beginning of the book. The young Snyder has just come down from his first ascent of Mount St. Helens and reads the reports of Hiroshima and Nagasaki. He makes a vow: "By the power and beauty and permanence of Mt. St. Helens, I will fight this cruel and destructive power and those who would seek to use it, for all my life." Of course that was sixty years ago now. Although you put it in the book, you are clearly no longer that fifteen-year-old, wanting to fight. And yet in another sense you have never stopped engaging with the powers you identified then, although the focus has changed over the years. So I am interested in how, from a Buddhist point of view, or from your point of view, one takes on the problem, the disease that you recognized as a teenager. If "fighting" it in an opposi-tional, dualistic way could be a way of replicating it, what alternatives are there? More particularly, could you say something about what has happened to that early vow?

GARY SNYDER: That's a very large question. I'll just say a few words about the idea of the vow. I was moved at that age of fifteen to express a vow to fight against, to oppose, governments and powers, scientists, politicians, whoever would dare use, hope to use, nuclear weaponry in any way on earth. The shock and outrage that had provoked that was the destruction of Hiroshima and Nagasaki, not only the suffering of human beings but realizing that these bombs could destroy much of nature itself.

One could take such a vow literally and try to act on it for a whole life. What I found over the years was a growth in my understanding of what had happened and why it happened. I also had to learn what is actually possible in the world. But most important, I learned more about what it means to take a vow. I could say, "Well I tried. And it didn't work, did it? I've been living my life by this and I guess it didn't come to anything—in fact it's worse than ever!"

MARTIN: But?

SNYDER: Well I came to realize, no use being so literal. So I've measured my original intention against my ignorance and my gradual great understanding, all these years. I had no answers either. But I had questions. How did we get here? How can I not contribute to more war? And why is it, how is it, that so many fellow human beings on earth are apparently comfortable with it? I realized that there is also a war against nature. The biosphere itself is subject to a huger explosion by far than anything nuclear—the half-million-year-long slow explosion of human impact.

One of my tools has been my poetry, my art. My guide came to be Shakyamuni and all the other Buddhas. And my ally, my critic, old Doctor Coyote, who is not inclined to make a distinction between good and evil.

MARTIN: I suppose that by the end of *Danger on Peaks*, the

vow has become the Bodhisattva's vow to save all sentient beings.

SNYDER: The primary vow, the primal vow, is to save all sentient beings. Or to help all sentient beings. Or, as Dogen says, "I take a vow to help all sentient beings take a vow to save all sentient beings." And I'd add, "Let myself, let us, be saved by all beings."

MARTIN: The extra layer?

SNYDER: Yes, we don't take it because *we* can do it. All we can do is take the vow to help *others* also take it. So the vow turns over on itself and rolls onward in its karma. In the Shin Buddhism of Japan it's called the Hongwan, the primary—the original—cosmic vow. There are two huge temples in Kyoto called Hongwanjis, the East Hongwanji and the West Hongwanji. That is, the East Temple of the primary vow and the West Temple of the primary vow.

Now the primary vow was taken eons ago, absolutely eons ago, by some wandering girl or boy who was eventually to become Amitabha Buddha, and who said, "I take a vow to save *all* beings, however many lifetimes it takes." So that is the story of Amitabha, Amida, whose primary vow is still at work in the world: to save all beings, regardless of how long it takes. Then Dogen says, "Well—to help them save themselves."

This is the amazing Mahayana vision, which ultimately does not shrink from the disappearance of this universe either. Such a huge view. So, let's have a cup of tea and take note of the falling leaves. Whatever else I have to say on that is in a poem or two.

MARTIN: In my own writing I keep returning to questions about impermanence and continuity. What is impermanent? What continues? In one sense everything is changing into everything else and is impermanent, falling leaves. But in another sense there is continuity.

SNYDER: Well, there's continuity of impermanence. We know that.

MARTIN: It seems to me there are a couple of moments in the book when you hint at the possibility of a sense of continuity that is different from what one has come to expect in your work. I'm thinking of two beautiful poems, "Waiting for a Ride" and "The Acropolis Back When." In the past you've tended to write away from the habitual big focus on *self* that is such a feature of modern culture. So instead of lots of *I*, you'll situate personal experience in relation to the Big Flow, the big living system, the non-dual world, and so on, and there are plenty of Buddhist and ecological reasons for doing so. But here I'm noticing something a bit different among the familiar. Both poems imagine the idea of some long continuity, perhaps even personal continuity, beyond this particular life.

Words like: "Or maybe I will, much later / some far time walking the spirit path in the sky," or else "Lifetimes ago [. . .] I climbed it." What sort of continuity might this suggest?

SNYDER: When Allen, Peter, Joanne, and I were traveling together in India, I let myself imagine my way into the view of literal reincarnation. There's a faint glimpse you catch once in a great while of ancient relationships, of eras come round again, deep déjà vu. One can play with these, but it's dangerous to take them too lightly. Those are risky poems.

MARTIN: I suppose the idea of continuity in your writing is more often to do with the continuity of the wild, and our participation in it. In *Danger on Peaks*, there is that poem towards the end where you reflect on the human impact on the planet that you spoke about earlier: "we're loose on earth / half a million years / our weird blast spreading." But then the poem goes on to remember that in the long view, wildness is ineradicable and that wilderness inevitably returns, grows green again. That's the long view.

SNYDER: That's not actually terribly long. But there is a question about the long-term impact of the particular variety of human civilization we have right now, the developed-world variety of civilization. Truth is, human beings probably had little impact up till twenty or thirty thousand years ago, when they started setting fires everywhere to improve the landscape.

MARTIN: And the developed-world variety of that trend is a very recent experiment.

SNYDER: Yes. And as Tonto says, "Speak for yourself, white man." It is not that everybody on earth is involved in that. There are many cultures and societies and peoples on earth who stand aside from the recent destructive side of civilization. Many are not doing it even now. They're suffering from it as much as nature herself is suffering from the effects of it.

MARTIN: You see it as something that has a fairly limited period of duration?

SNYDER: Not that I hope for it, but it's very likely that the present energy-intensive high population society will have to crash from key shortages and from garbage-glut. People will go on, keep a lighter technology going, and bring back the walking routes. Tell stories and meditate. Grow lots of garlic.

Another approach is Robinson Jeffers's, who said, "I am an *in*humanist. Not an antihumanist, just an inhumanist. In the inhuman perspective, humans are a passing problem." We might ask, "Well what's lost? When human beings are gone, what's lost?" Is that something we should concern ourselves with?

MARTIN: Well what *is* lost? When you're writing in the last section of the book about the bombing of the Buddhas of Bamiyan by the Taliban, it seems to me that you're looking at a sense of the loss of those human artifacts that have been destroyed.

SNYDER: Yes, I'm seeing it as deep art. It is what some bold builders tried to do, making a human figure into rock. What a culture.

MARTIN: Making big things, beautiful things.

SNYDER: Yes, there are some cultures who make bold things, as the Chinese did on quite a scale, for a long period of time. All the rich, high civilizations tried it. In my Bamiyan poem I don't want to make more of it than to say, "Honor the dust." Dogen somewhere says, "The whole planet is the dust of the bones of the ancient Buddhas."

MARTIN: So what's the difference?

SNYDER: So, honor the dust.

MARTIN: If it's all bones of Buddhas, then surely we are thinking in a pretty vast timescale. I hear your point that it doesn't need a very long view to think about the end of industrial civilization, but in terms of what you're calling inhumanism, you're also situating things in a geological perspective, a very long time.

SNYDER: Truth is, it's not too useful to calibrate on too large a timescale for human affairs.

MARTIN: What sort of scale would you want to use?

SNYDER: A useful scale is the present moment. The present moment starts about 11,000 years ago. Probably has about the same time to go into the future.

MARTIN: Beginning with agriculture?

SNYDER: Holocene. Post-Pleistocene.

MARTIN: Post the last Ice Age.

SNYDER: That's a Northern Hemisphere perspective, that the Holocene is about 11,000 years old. I'm not sure how it applies in other parts of the world. This is the moment in planetary time of our present climate, the flora and fauna in their combinations just for now. It's the world in which we live. Are we living it well? Or are we not—in terms of what it is now?

MARTIN: That is interesting, because in Southern Africa where I come from, there was no glaciation at that time. So it's more diverse and the plants are older, and the continuities go back a lot further.

SNYDER: More continuous, probably. Different portions of the globe have their own sort of present moment, assuming that things are constantly changing, but also knowing that there's a certain stability there for a while. And that finite world is also where we challenge ourselves: what do we know?

MARTIN: Our finite capacities? The limits of what we are able to do?

SNYDER: The limits of who we are, and the limits of what our world is.

MARTIN: We personally, or we as a species?

SNYDER: Individually, personally. Also, whoever we are, as a family. But the very last two poems in *Danger on Peaks* push it to the point where you "go beyond" that. Like, you asked about Tārā. Tārā is not another version of the Earth Mother. She's not the mother of all beings. She's the mother of the Buddhas. She is the mother of beings who see *beyond* being. The Earth Mother, the mother of all beings, is the mother of birth and death. The mother of the Buddhas is the mother of those beings who see through birth and death. Some people would like to see a little bit toward what is *through* birth and death. And Tārā is represented as a virgin.

MARTIN: But a mother of those beings.

SNYDER: As I understand it, only the mother of the Buddhas, not the mother of beings. She's a different kind of mother. She's the mother of Wisdom, the mother of Wisdom and Compassion. She's not giving birth to beings. She's not even the mother of God, like Mary. She is also the same as Prajñā. The goddess Prajñā is represented exactly the same in the iconography. And Prajñā is also called the goddess Wisdom, "who is the mother of the Buddhas."

MARTIN: And it's the Wisdom that goes beyond, *Mahāprajñāpāramitā*.

SNYDER: Yes. I'd say she is the mother of nondual insight, beyond birth and death. So she can look like a virgin if she wants. It doesn't matter. Or like a young woman. Actually, she's just portrayed as a very young woman in the iconography.

MARTIN: Or even like the world, the nondual world? The other day when I was walking with a friend from San Francisco up Steep Ravine on Mt. Tamalpais through that wonderful green forest, I imagined we were walking in the body of Tārā. But perhaps you'd say it's more like the body of Gaia—if we're going to talk in archetypes at all.

SNYDER: Yes? Dogen would also say it's the body of all the old dead Buddhas.

MARTIN: All those bones.

SNYDER: Sort of archaeological, geological. Or it is just the present moment happening.

MARTIN: We don't need to turn it into a metaphor.

SNYDER: Mt. Tamalpais is a very fine place.

MARTIN: And so close to the city. We have the same sort of situation where I live in Cape Town.

SNYDER: What's that mountain called?

MARTIN: Table Mountain. It really changes the sense of a city to have the wild mountain in the midst.

SNYDER: Tom Killion and I are working on a book on Mt. Tamalpais. He's a woodblock artist, and he's been doing some blocks of the Mt. Tamalpais area. He and I are doing some writing to go with that, and then there's "The Circumambulation [of Mt. Tamalpais]," the older stories, the native Miwok stories about it, and so forth. We're really focusing on its closeness to the city.

MARTIN: And the sea, sea and mountain and city, that combination. It's extraordinary, and it's something I recognize from home.

SNYDER: Yes, it's wonderful.

MARTIN: Gary, to go back to Tārā or Prajnā as mother of nondual insight, of Wisdom and Compassion. Could you connect these Buddhist images with Coyote? You said at the beginning that Coyote was your ally and so on. He's also nondual, isn't he? He isn't interested in those dualisms either.

SNYDER: No, he's not. How Doctor Coyote fits into this is a good question. In fact, that is one of the things about the Trickster figure: the Trickster manages to stand outside of all these discourses. Indefinitely. We'll have to work on that eventually.

MARTIN: Could you say something more about it now? We

don't have Coyote in Africa, so I always feel that I'm missing some resonances.

SNYDER: In West Africa isn't Spider a Trickster figure? I know there is or was a San Trickster, Mantis. At any rate, it's the Trickster we're looking at—Coyote is just one incarnation (and one of the most remarkable). Jehovah is playing Trickster when he gets Abraham to almost sacrifice Isaac, and then slips a ram into the bushes. Let's not try to do more than this with Trickster for now.

MARTIN: Sure. But to take it sideways slightly, there's that poem in *Danger on Peaks* about Doctor Coyote consulting his turds, and then a couple of others about consulting the "old advisors." You describe a feeling of not knowing what to do, like "despair at how the human world goes down." And then, in the poem, you do this thing, you consult the fallen trees or the mountain or whoever it is, and some kind of response comes, some kind of healing insight, returning you to the present moment. Reading this makes me wonder about how one writes about non-human things in ways that seem to be telling a human story.

SNYDER: You just have to try. You can't be sure if it's fair or not. It takes a lot of nerve to do this stuff.

MARTIN: I'm not asking you to explain the poems. But when

you appeal to Mount St. Helens for help and there is a sense of a response, what is happening?

SNYDER: There are mysteries that come to us. I could give a kind of reasonable answer to your question, but that would make it slighter than it is.

MARTIN: Yes, I know. It's just that those are obviously key moments in the book.

SNYDER: It stands better as a question: "How is it that, 'If you ask for help it comes, but not in any way you'd ever know'?" Many people who read that have said to me, "That's *true.*" I don't ask them, "How do you know it's true?" I believe they know. It's true for them. There is a truth there, but it's not a truth that everybody recognizes until it happens to them. Some people never have the necessity, or the nerve, to even *ask* for help.

ENJOY IT WHILE YOU CAN

Kitkitdizze • *2010*

As Julia was switching on the recorder, fiddling with the controls,
Gary began reciting this poem:

> The intellect of man is forced to choose
> Perfection of the life, or of the work,
> And if it take the second must refuse
> A heavenly mansion, raging in the dark.
> When all that story's finished, what's
>   the news?
> In luck or out the toil has left its mark:
> That old perplexity an empty purse,
> Or the day's vanity, the night's remorse.

GARY SNYDER: William Butler Yeats.

JULIA MARTIN: Has Yeats been important for you?

SNYDER: He was one of the important poets that I read, along
    with Pound and Eliot and Williams, and to a somewhat

lesser degree Wallace Stevens. And then Yeats. Williams was easy to read. Pound was a hard teacher. And Eliot I came to appreciate more in later years than I did at the time. Wallace Stevens I did not like much at all in the beginning. But Yeats I was delighted by.

MARTIN: That sound, that ear, such a wonderful ear.

SNYDER: He has such a great ear. And such an intricate way of bringing meter in. Very original little metric turns and twists, and very original rhymes. And also just a plain original mind, informed, I guess, by all that occultism.

MARTIN: All that magic and Golden Dawn. If we're talking about the sound patterns of words: when you're working on a poem, to what extent is it your ear that's doing it?

SNYDER: Well, the first thing that counts in poetry is music. If it doesn't have music, it's not a poem. What sets poetry apart from prose is a really interesting question, especially if it's not in some traditional meter. Then what sets it apart from prose? Simply that the lines don't all go to the end of the page? Come on! So a person has to have an ear, there has to be an ear for the music of the language. And to have an ear for the music of the language, you have to know what music of the language means. Which means you have to know what the vowels of spoken English are, and a few things like that. But behind that is something that is less easy to describe or define, which is taste, and ear, and sensibility, and sensibility to the nuances of language. Robert Duncan said poetry must have two things, music and magic.

MARTIN: That's Yeats, of course.

SNYDER: Yeats certainly, yes. Both are very hard to define.

MARTIN: Sometimes I teach so-called creative writing. In that context, I find that to get students to hear, to listen to the words, and to say what it is that you're listening for, is very difficult.

SNYDER: It is difficult, really. Especially if they're graduate students, and they're already into writing their poems, and they think they know what they're doing. They're kind of obstreperous. Undergraduates are easier to teach poetry to. Graduate students want to make up their own mind.

MARTIN: Gary, you began by reciting that Yeats poem, and that took us into thinking about poetry and ear. But I'm wondering now why you did that, why that poem now. Has that been a real choice, something that has been meaningful for you? Perfection of the life, or of the work?

SNYDER: That little poem has long been a touchstone for me, a reminder of foolish dualism and of the need to get away from the false choice of either "life" or "work"—and the miserable lure of the idea of perfection. Art is never perfect.

MARTIN: Thank you, yes. To take a different direction, being here at Kitkitdizze makes me particularly aware of your writing on place. You've been one of the people who is defining what we understand by a long-term commitment to a place and a bioregional awareness.

SNYDER: You know, for you to say that (which I gratefully accept) is also a cultural admission of the fact that we are an unsettled and disenfranchised people.

MARTIN: Absolutely.

SNYDER: I mean, I'm nothing.

MARTIN: You've only been here forty years.

SNYDER: I'm nothing. My ancestors' bones are not buried here. What do I know? If you want to talk about place, the sense of place, or the placedness of human beings prior to the mid-nineteenth century, you're talking about something entirely different that we have almost no idea of.

MARTIN: Okay, I agree. But what you're doing is an attempt at some kind of reparation, turning things around?

SNYDER: Oh, it's just my choice. I made up my mind that I wanted to find some place where I'd settle down for the rest of my life. I didn't assume that the children would want to stay. And I don't assume—you can't make that assumption in the twenty-first century, in this world.

The other side of it is that we are capable of beginning now to think of the whole Planet Earth as our place—

which nobody was quite up to before. They didn't have quite that much information. But saying that is not to free people to say, "I am a citizen of Planet Earth, I am a member of this planet." They've got to prove it. It's too easy to say, "I am a citizen of the Cosmos, I live in the Universe, I am at home here . . . " Well, come on, kid, show me how you do it. So you still can only know place specifically.

MARTIN: In the particulars.

SNYDER: You have to know the particulars. *If* you can begin to talk about the particulars, you might then be able to get a sense of what a larger planetary space might ultimately be. So it does come down to starting out with particulars, and being engaged with them. And that's really hard to come by. With most people you have to just start right out with putting them on the map. You know, which direction is North? And then, what does North mean? What *is* North?

MARTIN: What does that question mean?

SNYDER: Which direction is North? What *is* North? That question means can you answer it, where is North?

MARTIN: Well, I know where it is on the map.

SNYDER: What is it in worldly terms? On the map it's just up.

MARTIN: Well, I know how the sun travels across the sky, and I get North in relation to that.

SNYDER: The East and West are created by the spinning of

the earth. The axis of rotation is what we call North and South. The projection of the axis of the rotation of the earth in the northern hemisphere is North. It happens to come out very close to a star. It's not quite on it, it's just off a little bit. But that's what North is. It's the axis of the turning of the earth, and measuring yourself against that.

MARTIN: So for us, where I come from, we need to know where South is.

SNYDER: Yes. The Southern Cross is even further off the axis. One time in northern Botswana, I was looking at the Southern Cross and actually pointed to the axis of it, like that, and took a line from the stars that were up over the horizon, so I knew where the North Pole was down under the ground. And then I knew that for sure I was on the planet. When I first landed in Japan, in 1956, they happened to have a clear night the first or second night I was there. And sure enough, I could recognize the constellations. So then I knew I was still at least on the same planet.

Well, those are what the local Palas are all about, the guardians of the Four Directions in Buddhism, and the importance of knowing what is meant by the guardians of the Four Directions. But in Buddhist East Asia they speak of Ten Directions: the four cardinal directions that we are acquainted with, plus the quarters (North-West,

South-East, and so on), plus Up and Down. That makes ten.

So some of the Buddhist recitations invoke all the Buddhas in the Ten Directions. And the Three Realms: the Realm of Form, the Realm of No-Form, and the Realm of Desire. We live in the Realm of Desire, being metabolic beings, whereas rocks are in the Realm of Form. They have no metabolism.

MARTIN: They just are.

SNYDER: That's what it seems.

MARTIN: And the Realm of No-Form?

SNYDER: Well, most people have never seen that. That's Arupa, No-Form. That's one of those things that when you get into trying to figure out Buddhist philosophy, you think, Now what do they mean by that? You can find commentaries that describe it, but they're not very helpful.

So the idea of how you locate yourself is interesting, those cosmic guidances that are given. And then there are the local guidances, which are always: Which way does the water flow? What's the watershed? Where's the river going? The mountains are that way, it's downhill that way . . . you sort of orient yourself. The watershed is a great way to orient yourself.

MARTIN: And do you think that understanding the particularities of one location enables you then to extend that further?

SNYDER: Well, then you know at least what you're looking at. Otherwise you wouldn't have ever noticed, no matter where you are. You know what to look around for, and what questions you want to ask. The next step that's important for people is knowing what the plant life is.

MARTIN: There's been a certain criticism of the literature associated with place-based bioregionalism, which says that in North America it sometimes gets too parochial, too insular, too disconnected from the global. But in your work, I think, you can't make that division. The particularity is there, but if you're going to think ecologically at all, you're going to think interpenetration and flows, and the particular manifesting the global.

SNYDER: Yeah, but you know for a lot of people that doesn't do a damn bit of good.

MARTIN: Explain?

SNYDER: Because most issues are more local than that. Like the timber issues here are the issues that belong to mountains (that is to say, there is a fast runoff of the rain), issues that belong to a summer-dry, winter-wet climate, which changes what you can do. And you have to be much more careful in a summer-dry climate because when the winter rains come, they cause a lot of quick erosion in the sense that the ground has totally dried out, and you can lose your forest. In a few decades you can have lost enough soil that you can never get your trees back. That's what happened to Greece and to a lot of other parts of the Mediterranean. That's how they lost their forest. They cut too many trees down, and it was impossible for them to regrow because of the rainfall washing out the soils. Plus goats.

MARTIN: After the goat, the desert, they say. They eat everything.

SNYDER: Yeah. And they eat the young trees. They can eat grass and it will grow back.

So I don't know what the criticism of place is, except a misguided criticism from urban people who are educated and don't understand that they live in a place or that it matters.

MARTIN: I think it's saying that yes, of course, we need to rediscover our locatedness in place, but that global flows and patterns—political, social, economic, and so on—are inextricably part of where we are as well.

SNYDER: Nobody argues that. But everybody knows those things already and don't know anything about the place. So it's not a fair argument, because a lot of people haven't even given place a start in their thinking. They just come in already with, you know, Western Civ on their minds, and they think that place is for the peasant—the *paysan*, the person of the land, the person of the place.

MARTIN: The other day when I was flying here, a daytime flight from London to San Francisco, it was a wonderful thing to travel over the surface of the planet, see it all for a change from that perspective, that big view—the mountains, the rivers, lakes, fields, forest fires. The world. I kept thinking about your essay on Dogen's "Mountains and Waters Sutra" in *The Practice of the Wild* and also, of course, *Mountains and Rivers Without End*. It does seem to me that you do it beautifully there: a big view of the whole phenomenal world continually arising, all of it seen as mountains and rivers, a nondual view.

SNYDER: Well, that's one of the things I'm trying to do, yes. Did you go over Greenland? Isn't that remarkable?

MARTIN: It is remarkable.

SNYDER: The first time I flew over Greenland, I realized that I hadn't known how many rocky mountains there were. Big mountains.

MARTIN: Yes. And even before that, the coast of Scotland was so extraordinary, a very ragged, wild coast, so many inlets. When we finally got to San Francisco, my initial feeling after all those hours of mountains and rivers and sky was quite negative. Kind of: oh no, look at all these grids that the humans have built. But then the pattern of it all was really so *interesting*, a fascinating thing this human mind has made, this world of San Francisco.

SNYDER: Or any place.

MARTIN: Or any place, but that was where I was. So I realized again how easy it is, initially, to love the so-called undeveloped environments of a continent, and to feel a kind of repugnance towards its cities. But actually seeing the patterns of San Francisco from the air, it all looked so intelligent, lively, beautiful even. It reminded me of that poem from *Mountains and Rivers*, "Walking the New York Bedrock," where even that city of cities is in a curious sense a natural formation.

So one does have that sense sometimes that all of it is really mountains and rivers. But can you say something about maintaining such a view?

SNYDER: Well, the watershed goes through cities.

MARTIN: "Rivers that never give up."

SNYDER: Yeah, for one thing. All cities are part of some natural conformation of the wild, and they are adapted to the conformation of the land. And they are where they are for some human reason. San Francisco is where you can bring a ship in out of the ocean, and where a great part of the drainage of California comes out into San Francisco Bay, a huge, huge watershed (the San Joaquin Valley to the south, Sacramento Valley to the north). All that is coming out into San Francisco Bay. It's been mistreated a lot, and the gold-mining they did up here shallowed the bay considerably, but they are still able to get aircraft carriers in, just barely.

To think about cities, you think a little bit about the idea of the mandala, and the uses of human habitation and the possibilities of different sets and structures of habitation, and the infrastructure that brings water and takes waste away, and so forth. It's not simple. It's better done some places than others, but there have been some intelligent and magical—deliberately magically intended—constructions of concentrations of population.

However, it would be a mistake to think that all human accomplishment comes out of those concentrations. What the intervening lands offer, each in their own way, are particular lessons, including the places that are not suitable habitat for any economy other than hunters and gatherers—they just won't work for pasture or for agriculture. Like much of the Great Basin of western Turtle Island.

MARTIN: Right.

SNYDER: I talked a little bit about that in *The Practice of the Wild*, that every region does actually have its own particular wilderness, which is the wildest place in that area, the least-known place, the place where you can gather wild herbs, the place where the bears are, the place where you go for magic, the place where you go to be alone. There are two things that are really educational. One is being with a bunch of really smart people. The other is being all by yourself.

MARTIN: So cities are in a sense mandalas, and there is wildness even in the city. On the other hand, for me the point arises that in order to focus critique, one may also need to define a particular action or orientation as problematic.

SNYDER: Oh that is so . . . French! There is some truth in that, yes.

MARTIN: What I am saying is that from one point of view it's all mountains and waters, a nondual world, not-two. In Buddhism they might talk about an absolute view. But at the same time, of course, there are other ways of seeing, or focal settings, that might need to see things differently. If you hope to be able to *change* something, or critique something, or overturn something, then you need to be able to identify what the problem is. And a city may well, to some extent, be manifesting that problem.

SNYDER: Well, everything has its problems. Problems are only a human idea anyway. And yeah, sure, everything is problematic. If you want to have a problem, there'll be a problem.

MARTIN: I'm thinking in particular of environmental issues.

SNYDER: There's only one dualism that counts: Being and Non-Being. When they're talking about dualism, that's what they're talking about.

MARTIN: Explain?

SNYDER: Everything boils down to either it exists or it doesn't exist. That's dualism.

MARTIN: That's the real dualism, and the others are all constructs?

SNYDER: It's all ecology otherwise. It's all interactions.

MARTIN: But if you want to take on an exploitative, profiteering, capitalist . . .

SNYDER: Well, maybe the capitalists are the good guys. I mean, Stalin was a murderer.

MARTIN: But you know what I'm saying, Gary.

SNYDER: Sweden is full of corruption. . . . But just to go back to Buddhism, Hinduism, basic philosophies, when they want to really get down on it, it's Being/Non-Being that they're really dealing with. An ultimate human sense of dualism. Hence *mu:* Does a dog have Buddha-nature? Without. That means Non-Being, that's the character for Non-Being. And then in the commentary on the Wu-Men Kuan it says, "Being? Non-Being? Being? Non-Being?" And then it goes on. Presence? Absence? Form? Emptiness?

So it's just good to remember that that's really what

counts, what the fundamental territory of investigation is, if one wants to feel hung up.

MARTIN: That's the point of entry?

SNYDER: You might as well go all the way . . . to really be hung up.

MARTIN: And someone like your dog, Emi? "Beasts got the Buddha-nature / all but Coyote"?

SNYDER: That's a line I wrote, yeah. But then you've got to go into the question of old Doctor Coyote.

MARTIN: What about Emi?

SNYDER: Well, that's her problem.

MARTIN: And Doctor Coyote?

SNYDER: Old Doctor Coyote. Well, you know who that is.

When I was in Australia with Nanao in 1981 or so, he was interviewed on Australian radio about Zen. The interviewer asked him, "Tell me about what kind of Zen you teach, Mr. Sakaki." And Nanao said, "Oh, I represent a very interesting, special kind of Zen. It is called Fox Zen. Trickster Zen."

MARTIN: Would you say that is your department as well?

SNYDER: No, not really. No. But the Japanese Buddhists enjoy the idea of Trickster Zen as much as they enjoy anything else. Though they also warn against teachers who are foxes because they'll present themselves as more enlightened than they are.

MARTIN: And could be quite manipulative with it, misleading.

SNYDER: Could be. More trouble than it's worth. But then there are also some Zen phrases that say, "Old Golden Face has just caused heaps of entangling vines. We've all been tricked by him." Meaning, the Buddha. What do they mean by that? Oh, well we've got to work on that! More tangling vines.

There's a story of how one old Zen master's disciples came to him in private and he said to him, "Master, I have a problem." The master said, "You have a problem. Okay. Bring it up at the next general meeting." So at the next general meeting, the master called the monk and said, "Please come forward." Then he said to everyone, "Assembly, here is a monk with a problem." And sent him back.

MARTIN: That's it?

SNYDER: Yes. You know, part of that is, everybody has a problem, has problems. They are not always the problems that spiritual practice can clarify.

Anyway, to get back to place and bioregionalism: the ambition of bioregionalism is not a huge or exotic ambition. It is simply the hope that people will pay attention, for starters, to where they are. And to remind them that nature happens locally. If you want to study nature, you only have to go outside the door. Wherever you are, it is something specific and close to you. Even when it looks far away, it's close to you. If you're looking at mountain sheep on a mountain ten miles away, that's not that far away.

It's not a huge question, *except* (and this is largely for bureaucrats and local people) it's overlooked. And it should not remain as simply the domain of the scientists. It is one of the domains that all of us need to be present in, rather than dividing it up between culture and science. Environmentalism brings us to really understanding that environmental issues are not solved just by science alone. They're solved by feeling, by art, by artists, by everyone who is involved in it in one way or another. It's not just economics.

MARTIN: I agree. Yes. Over the years I've come back many times to your sense of wildness, like in that first essay in *The Practice of the Wild*—that wilderness places may dwindle, but wildness is ineradicable.

SNYDER: Well, wildness is process. It's just a name for the process of the impermanence and constant flow of change of phenomena, as constantly going on without human intervention. That is wild process. It's a simple insight, really.

MARTIN: Simple is useful.

SNYDER: And it's good to remind ourselves and others that we are all, as we are right now, the result of that process acting out. The whole of evolutionary change and development took place without a plan or a schedule. It was not drawn up by engineers or planners. It comes about by its own dynamics, and those dynamics are complex, but they are in some ways understandable. And those are what we call wild, the dynamics of wildness.

I had this conversation several times with the supervisor of the Tahoe National Forest, whom I used to have breakfast with from time to time. He was so focused on management and what he called treatments. And he said, "Well we can't just let the forest alone. We've done too much to it already, so we have to keep doing things to it." I said, "Well that's just an argument for annual budget."

MARTIN: Did they listen to you?

SNYDER: They appreciated what I said, but they're not going to give up getting their budget.

MARTIN: To change direction a bit, as I said before, being here at Kitkitdizze brings to mind your work on place. But sitting here in your house surrounded by so many tools and made things also suggests the idea of craftsmanship, and your appreciation of work done with care, with tools, not always by hand. From that there's an analogy with writing. But first, why is good craftsmanship important?

SNYDER: Oh, you know the answer to that. So why are you asking me?

MARTIN: Because I want you to say it!

SNYDER: Actually, craftsmanship is just a variety of mindfulness. Mindfulness is what's important.

MARTIN: Wherever it is applied.

SNYDER: I don't know why it's important. Probably it isn't always important. But doing things attentively, being able to see what you're doing, and be conscious of how your mind is working is also being conscious of how you use your body, and what your tools are. So you start out by learning to tie your shoes and learning to put your little drawers on.

MARTIN: Taking care.

SNYDER: And it goes from there that you can take care of yourself, and then you can take care of others. And then you can take pleasure in that. And there is a sense of self-confidence, of competence, that arises in knowing for yourself that you've done something well. That permeates all the crafts, and a lot of other things. And it's what might make it possible for a person to be a completely wise, happy, and enlightened accountant. Because they say, I know how to do this, I'm doing it right each time.

MARTIN: And I'm present in it.

SNYDER: And I'm present in it, exactly. You know, for mindfulness, repetition is not necessarily an enemy. Because every time you do something it's different. That's a very interesting discovery. I learned that doing Buddhist ritual over and over again, chanting in particular, and realizing that it was never the same twice, and that I was still learning new things after quite a few years. That's one of the interesting things about ceremony. Being too interested in always having things new and interesting is to miss the point. That's why it's fun to go to Noh drama.

MARTIN: You know what's going to happen.

SNYDER: You know what's going to happen, but it doesn't happen the same way. So that's one of the great strengths of performance and art, and it's why you don't have to have a different story every time. It's the presentation that counts as much as what the story is supposed to be. It's what the artist brings to it in a new way. That's what musical performance does. So that's true of a lot of things. What we call a bad electrician or a bad plumber is somebody who hasn't paid attention, and hasn't maybe learned what some of the details are.

MARTIN: What you're saying about repetition reminds me of that essay in *The Practice of the Wild* where you're talking about the idea of originality, and how in certain cultural contexts it's just fine to be making the same kind of vessel that your master has made. And maybe one day someone comes along and does something different, but that's not so much the point.

SNYDER: Yeah, there I was talking about the nature of the traditional Japanese practice and understanding of craft and apprenticeship, and the idea that we don't need a great deal of creativity. We need attention to doing things well, and then somebody creative will come along sooner or later.

MARTIN: And now we've turned it the other way, so that people have to constantly be trying to do something new.

SNYDER: Well, you know Japan is pretty much the same now. The mentality of our current age is almost totally uncritically focused on the idea of newness, of innovation, of technology moving on, of technology bringing new money to the economy and new pleasure to our lives. And so far, very few people have pointed out that this cannot go on forever, and it's kind of a trap.

MARTIN: So as a writer, how do these ideas about craftsmanship and mindfulness relate to your own work?

SNYDER: Well, language is one of the more fluid and unpredictable things in the world, and it's very difficult to investigate our natural languages to the bottom. In fact you can't. So it's partly a case, like all of the arts, I think, of opening yourself to the unexpected, and allowing yourself to be surprised. And it's a balance between having mastered the skills and being open to the unpredictable. That's the difference between a straightforward craftsperson and an artist.

MARTIN: So as a poet, you're saying be open to surprise and the unexpected, while being educated in the tradition.

SNYDER: Yes, but not all poems do that. Meanwhile, there's a lot of other work that needs to be done with poetry, and with writing: addressing "problems," and expressing this or that aspect of the world and the story that you're in. And then, once in a great while, a poem kind of creeps from around a corner, comes in from the other side, and you slip it in with your work.

MARTIN: So they're all serving different purposes.

SNYDER: There are many purposes. A kids' jingle is one purpose.

MARTIN: That poem about mushrooms—"Don't ever eat Boletus / If the tube-mouths they are red."

SNYDER: We all know various little rhymes like that: "Sedges have edges / Rushes are round / Grasses have joints from the top to the ground." I learned that years ago and I still use it.

MARTIN: So the poems in any collection of yours are going to serve quite an array of purposes. In terms of your priorities now for writing and thinking, do you see a continuity with where you've come from? Are there similar themes?

SNYDER: I think it's been pretty consistent, that in some ways it's been a simple and consistent message. But the simple and consistent messages are sometimes the hardest ones to get across.

MARTIN: I can intuit what you mean, but could you say more about it—I imagine if one went back to that Haida myth thesis you wrote as a student, you might find things that you're still talking about now.

SNYDER: Could be, that's true. And I have never felt needy about writing or being a writer. I'm content to quit any time.

MARTIN: Needy in the sense of "I need to be a writer"?

SNYDER: Yes. "I need to write more, etc. I need to do more." That seems like another kind of trap. So periodically I get engaged in taking care of other things, and that feels just as good; it's just as important.

What is much in my consciousness now (and it would be)—more than it used to be—is impermanence. As Gore Vidal said, "I'm nearing the Exit." And as Billy Budd said (Philip Whalen's quote), being sentenced to the gallows certainly makes you pay attention. So I find myself being attentive in a new way, which is the attention that you have to have when you realize your time is not limitless.

I can also say to myself, Well, I've done a lot. And I'll leave a lot undone so that other people will be able to do it too. How it all looks later is not my business. People will do what they do with it, whatever. So that's kind of freeing. It frees you up.

I've got two writing projects going after I finish straightening out the legalities of our land use here. My "Dharma Memoir" (just a working title), for which I have a lot of notes and anecdotes. It's going to be . . .

MARTIN: Provocative?

SNYDER: It's going to be provocative, if nothing else.

The other is . . . Well, Bruce Boyd is a neighbor of mine, and he was on the crew of people who helped build this house. He's an architect now. He and I are going to write a little account of the building of this house in the summer of 1970. As process. As process with young people, many of whom were totally inexperienced, and as process with the stated goal of using as much local material as possible, no power tools, doing things all in the old way.

MARTIN: How long did it take?

SNYDER: Three months, working full-time.

MARTIN: And how many people?

SNYDER: About fifteen. Everyone camped here.

MARTIN: What a wonderful thing.

SNYDER: It was a wonderful summer. Everybody took turns cooking, and everybody took turns being a carpenter. So the young women rotated through the crew in all ways, and the men all rotated through in all ways. Everybody who was on that crew said it was the best summer of their lives. Many still say that.

MARTIN: What a pleasure.

SNYDER: Back in those days we didn't wear so much clothes either. It was summer and everybody was young.

MARTIN: And children?

SNYDER: Kai and Gen were babies. Kai was about two and a half, running around, and Gen wasn't quite a toddler yet. I don't think there were any other little kids around, though kids came through because we had a lot of guests. But we scheduled our life here so that our off days were Wednesday and Thursday, and weekends we worked. That way, when the guests came, we could put them to work.

MARTIN: Otherwise they might have thought it was a holiday camp.

SNYDER: Yes.

MARTIN: So (and this reminds me of that Yeats poem that you began with), you've never said to yourself, in an exclusive sense, "I am a poet." You tend to do many things, including writing, and writing may be various kinds of writing.

SNYDER: That's been my way of being a poet. I don't think it is wise to make one's sole idea of life and career as an artist. That makes you less of an artist, at least in poetry. There are some kinds of art, like being a musician, where all you have to do is practice, practice, practice.

MARTIN: It's tough that, yes.

To rewind to what you said earlier about nearing

the Exit, and about reflecting on impermanence, as one would, as one must: you're undeniably an elder now. One couldn't argue with that—

SNYDER: I wouldn't argue.

MARTIN: So what can you say to the rest of us from that perspective?

SNYDER: I can't say anything to all of you.

MARTIN: Okay, to me.

SNYDER: So what's your question?

MARTIN: It's about old age, sickness, and death.

SNYDER: Old age, sickness, and death? Enjoy it while you can! Because soon you won't even have that.

MARTIN: Thank you, Gary.

SNYDER: It's like a young fellow I knew who wrote me from the monastery in Kyoto years ago. I had returned to this country, and he had just entered the Daitoku-ji monastery as a monk. He had been there for about a year, and he wrote to me: "Hey, Gary, what do you do about this celibacy?" And I wrote back, "Enjoy it while you can." Ten years later, I got a letter from him in Texas, and he said, "You know, you were right!"

MARTIN: On a related track, do you think it actually works to find an analogy between the Buddhist remedy for personal suffering (I'm thinking of the narrative of the Four Noble Truths) and a response to ecosocial suffering? Can one usefully draw that analogy—between an individual impulse of clinging and grasping and a social ideology of limitless material accumulation, endless growth, massive consumption, and so on?

SNYDER: Yes, you can, but that's a Western thing to do. I've used the term "institutionalized greed." It's not only that we have these problems, but that they have been institutionalized in a way to make them look positive in some of our societies. So that just adds to the difficulty. But it doesn't necessarily tell us something about human nature. That's a slightly different question.

MARTIN: What I'm wondering is whether the response to suffering at a personal level in terms of Buddhist practice is something that can in fact be applied at a more social level.

SNYDER: A lot of people in the world have said this: a problem is your problem when it's on your back, when it's laid at your door, and you must deal with that. If you can deal with the problems that are right in your front yard, you're doing all right. So avoid getting excited about abstractions when there are often things that are much more immediate.

Households do, in small ways, discover new ways to be in the world. I know one that is now saying, "We're not giving each other new things anymore. We're giving each other things that we already had ourselves that we didn't use." Or they're finding things at the Goodwill that they can use, or in other ways recycling things, not adding new things into the mix. It's very smart. You've got books in your library that are really worthwhile, and you really love, but you also know that you don't need them anymore, and they can be gifts to people. And so forth. That's just one little thing in the sense of what can you do that's right at your front door.

But that's not the only answer, of course. And every day we know things that we need to be doing on a larger social level. But it's still just sweeping the garden.

MARTIN: Any size.

SNYDER: Yes. As my teacher Oda Roshi said. Just on a larger scale. But it's not that you should allow it to enlarge your sense of what you're doing that much. Writing a letter to the president is just writing a letter. You could also be writing a letter to the local sheriff. It's equal in a certain way. And the local sheriff will probably pay more attention.

Well, okay. The most interesting thing I said today was: "Old age, sickness, and death—enjoy it while you can."

And there you are, right up against Being and Non-Being. When you have old age, sickness, and death, you are still in Being. You're not in Non-Being. So what's the difference?

SELECTED **LETTERS**

October 24, 1983

Dear Gary Snyder,

During this year I've been working on a thesis which involves looking at your work. I've meant for a long time to write to you, telling you how much I like what you write, and asking some questions. But I haven't done so, because I've felt that a letter should say something particularly significant. Now this one doesn't really, but it's a letter nevertheless. Would you mind commenting on some ideas that I've been thinking about? Obviously, this is not intended to be an interrogation—it would be excellent, though, to have your comment on some of these issues.

Recently I have been working in the first tiny antinuclear group in South Africa: a relatively new concern here—the first power station to come on stream soon. But one is rather isolated—difficult not to feel that the big ideas are happening elsewhere, that the country is understandably a pariah to the rest of the world, and that involvement in anything other than eradication of this apartheid system is irrelevant.

Now your work provided a context for my recognition that the many different areas of my concern are not usefully separable, as well as a renewal of the directive to *see* that I first encountered in William Blake. Thank you.

I tend to be suspicious of the value of thesis-writing, as of involvement in academia, but having been given time and money to do this, it seems the appropriate next step. So I'm using the thesis as a way of exploring a number of questions that are important to me, doing the reading that I've wanted to do for a long time, and drawing some tentative conclusions that may be useful to someone else. My original interest was in the language people have used to describe what may be called an experience of epiphany, and the problems involved in this expression, and this as a way into looking at the implications and viability of different orientations towards this kind of experience. Related to this is my fascination with the movements in American youth culture of the 1950s, '60s, early '70s and their extraordinary search for transcending experience, cleansing the doors of perception, etc. . . . I was far too young at the time, but always intrigued: watching the South African repercussions of it all with vicarious delight. So—given all this, your work seemed a good place to start.

In a paper I gave recently to other MA students, I looked at some of your work in the context of a question I overheard at a poetry reading earlier this year: "Why do apolitical people always write Nature Poetry?," suggesting that the orientation towards nature that your work represents is, potentially at least, a politically radical one. I discussed this in terms of the Ecology movement (E. F. Schumacher, André Gorz, etc.) and the feminist concern with identifying and eradicating "patriarchal" modes of consciousness, claiming that you attempt to establish a number of disparate concerns as part of the same issue. I said that because Western technological society represents such an overkill on the side of those values associated with patriarchy, you emphasise the necessity of incorporating the "feminine" in consciousness, Nature in Culture, drawing it seems to me to quite a large extent on the Jungian association of this with the Unconscious. What does this sound like to you?

And now from this some questions: please comment on whatever seems interesting to you—

I've been particularly interested in your affirmation of the Goddess: Who is she? When I gave the paper, the feminists in the group were rather wary of your point of view—"Isn't he in fact perpetuating the old male myth that associates women with nature, the body, etc.? To what extent is he really getting away from that sort of attitude?" What is your reaction to that? I'm not sure that the question wasn't tinged somewhat with the assumption which says that men are more or less by definition disqualified from a valid feminist viewpoint. . . . A very interesting book that I've just read about women writers on spiritual quests (Carol Christ, *Diving Deep and Surfacing*) shows that a number of feminist writers adopt, as an alternative to the patriarchal stress on "spiritual transcendence," a way that includes precisely the same sort of identification with Nature, the body, emphasis on "immanence," etc., and consequent metaphors of descent that I see in your work. Adrienne Rich, for example, writes about the need for "Diving into the Wreck" which is the dark underside of the patriarchal world, diving down beneath culture and its values in search of a new vision. Very reminiscent of *Turtle Island*.

Now this sounds of course very much like Jung—to what extent would you say your work is informed by the Jungian paradigm? And what, if any, do you consider its limits to be? And what do you understand by the term "androgyny"?

The reason I ask is that I've been reading back numbers of *The Journal of Transpersonal Psychology*—several contributors claim that it is too easy to assume compatibility between Western and Buddhist models of consciousness because of the implied dualism in the Western model, which can't really deal with nondualistic experiences. What does this sound like?

Another question: One of my most important teachers has been Blake, and so in reading your work I seem to find a fair amount of Blakean resonance—but I'm not sure how much is just my reading of it. So, what are your comments on this? And what about the other Romantics—Wordsworth? Coleridge? To what extent would you say that your work is a response to / reaction against the assumptions implicit in the Leavisite critical tradition and those of Modernist poetry?

And now I suppose (for me) the most important questions: About "epiphany"—in an early comment in *Earth House Hold*, you describe the culture's dependence on sporadic moments of sex and the industry of Romantic love for any experience of epiphany that most people are likely to have. Is the term still useful to you? And what does it mean? What do you make of Maslow's distinction between "peak experiences" and "plateau experiences" (the latter a "unitive consciousness," which is a *constant*—rather than climactic— simultaneous perception of the sacred and the ordinary, the miraculous and the ordinary . . .)?

And now, What is the relation between epiphany and the *Goddess*?

- To what extent has it been necessary to redefine the popular expectations of what epiphany may mean?

- Is the opposition of "transcendence" vs. "immanence" useful here?
- How does this relate to the writing of nature poetry?
- How can nature poetry be politically radical?
- How have the expectations of what nature poetry is about had to be redefined?

And finally, what does the term "patriarchal" mean to you?

So this is the end of my questions—too many I know, but some you may find interesting. I'm aware certainly of the ultimate irrelevance of all this verbalising—but it seems to be an unavoidable part of writing a thesis.

Thank you very much,

Yours,

Julia Martin

"One thought fills immensity."

Now, as I reread this letter, the tone seems rather formal and wordy—difficult to know what register to adopt when writing to someone you don't know. I'll temper this by sending you some colours and some cloth—designed and printed by Zulu people in Natal. I found it on my last visit there. . . . What do you think of e.e. cummings?

January 3, 1984

Dear Julia,

Now it's the new year, the sun has come out for two days in a row after two dark months and forty inches of rain, and I'm catching up a bit on mail. Your long and interesting letter came right on the heels of reading an essay that Sherman Paul (University of Iowa, English Department, Iowa City) has recently written on me. It's not published yet, but he touches on many of the same concerns and questions that you do. Also, a book on my work has just come out—*Gary Snyder's Vision: Poetry and the Real Work,* by Charles Molesworth (A Literary Frontiers Edition, University of Missouri Press, Columbia, 1983)—which is specifically about the politics implicit and explicit in my poetry and prose. It's a short-sighted, historically ignorant notion that some people might have that "nature poetry" is apolitical. I think in *The Real Work* I pointed out that it is one of the functions of poetry, and indeed of art, to present the nonhuman; this presentation, when authentic, is political in its very challenge of the assumptions of anthropocentricism and therefore of all orders of hierarchy and domination in human society. My work is clearly radical in the tradition of anarchism, first, and in the post-Marxist decentralist critique of all forms of statism, second. The Buddhist dimension is in a way further exploration of that. There are both political and psychological (as well as historical) reasons for bringing in the "feminine."

So, the Goddess, and your question who is she? First, she is a real historic and prehistoric personage in our deep culture-minds. It is not just a male myth that associates women with nature . . . it's also an old female myth. One has only to look at the anthropological evidence and note also that a very strong wing of the feminist movement today with its reaffirmation of goddess worship, witchcraft, and the linking of the women's / goddess movement to a women's international ecology movement as evidence. Of course, I'm influenced by Jung, and much more: In fact, way back in the fifties I did a brief critique of the dangers and errors in the Jungian method. Jane Ellen Harrison, Sir James Frazer, Robert Graves, Frederick Engels, and other classics of anthropology and history informed my early view. It gets interesting to me, when I move beyond those Neolithic, proto-patriarchal figures either into the Paleolithic, which is probably a relatively gender-free male / female playground; or into the strong psychology and epistemology of Mahayana Buddhism and the light use of gender metaphors in the language of compassion and wisdom. So that the goddess Prajnā is an image and metaphor of transcendent wisdom. You might look into Tibetan

Buddhism for the development of a goddess metaphor that really transcends gender or "male myth."

Blake has not been all that important to me, and less so all the other Romantics. Pound was for me more of an instructor, and in another way, Jeffers and Lawrence. But most usefully perhaps, a combination of readings in American Indian and other pre-literate literatures, and Chinese poetry.

Now, you are getting really close to things when you ask what the relation between epiphany and the Goddess is. Epiphany is that moment when you become one with something. The swoop of a bird, the sound of the rain, the clack of a broken tile, peach blossoms. And also, another human being. But in Zen language, we don't exploit the sexual metaphor, because the kind of oneness I am speaking of here—that is nondualistic and depends neither on human or the nonhuman—is far deeper than sexual love, and the metaphor of sexual love as "oneness with the divine" is misleading. Sexual love is simply—as a rule—its own kind of oneness, for its own delightful outcome and purposes. So, if the metaphor of the Goddess is very useful at all, it is (as the Buddhists use it) as that image of the world . . . Maya . . . that seduces us to the very point and purpose of causing us to transcend it / her. Illusion and wisdom are one in the territory of this mystery. That woman, or the Goddess, should be projected as image of illusion / wisdom here is probably a male-derived metaphor. If you want to look at a set of women's metaphors, look at the lore and literature of Shiva, a male deity of considerable phallic prowess, who is clearly much worshipped by women in India and who serves as a vehicle for *their* transcendence.

As for immanence, my sense of that is in the actualization of the bodhisattva's vow that insight be carried into action, that the world be moved in as sacramental. The world as lived in by subsistence-level people is also sacramental, and the accomplishment of transcendent insight is not necessary to dancing properly in the universe. It is perhaps a special need in postcivilized times. So, if there is something left unclear here, I suggest you look at *The Real Work*—if you haven't already—to pick up the loose ends. "How can nature poetry be politically radical" as and through all of the above.

"Patriarchal" means, to me, a society in which in the power balance the males have a preponderance of *say* in all kinds of decision making and wielding of authority. I doubt that there was ever a true "matriarchy"—there have been plenty of societies with a rough gender-power balance, I think. True patriarchy is a function of civilization and the accumulation of wealth, most likely. In the many thousands of cultures around the world, you cannot generalize too much, but in my thinking of gender politics I would be careful always to avoid hasty criticisms of other cultures and their outward appearances, whose inward workings we don't yet understand.

Traditional Australian Aboriginal women—as I have experienced—have been very resilient and tough in their defense of their own culture against criticisms leveled at it by Australian feminists. And there is and should be a division of labor, because nobody can be an expert at everything: the point is that the load of labor and its rewards and prestige be roughly equal. Ivan Illich's recent books *Shadow Work* and *Gender* are very illuminating, and somewhat controversial, on these matters.

So here is a somewhat formal and wordy response to yours. I enjoy doing this, because you clearly have thought through many of the same paths I have, and so we are stepping through the paces together here, and how would I ever have thought I'd hear from you there clear off in South Africa? Warm regards and comradely feelings from here to there. My two sons, Kai—fifteen and Gen—thirteen, and my wife Masa greet you.

Gary Snyder

I'll be sending you a copy of my new book of poems sea mail. The Goddess is on the cover . . .

February 6, 1984

Dear Gary,

I have been so happy to read and reread your kind and interesting letter: So good to feel that there is another human out there with whom contact has been made. I do find it extraordinarily difficult to work in semi-isolation here, with nobody around who has really shared the same concerns. Thank you very much. And thank you for sending a copy of *Axe Handles*. [. . .]

I'm working on a paper for one of our antinuclear information packages that you might find interesting: an attempt to suggest some connections. (I imagine that all that antinuke work can do here is to help start making connections between apparently separate areas of concern—the machinery of repressive legislation prevents much other protest.) This paper will look at some of the connections between women, "nature," the colonised, and animals: how in the oppositional relations set up by dualistic thinking, they all end up on the wrong side of the fence, along with "emotion," "intuition," etc., in a society which celebrates rationality, "culture," the "masculine," the human, and so on. One useful response to this general exploitation seems to be an attempt to reinstate the mythology of the Goddess, as many people (although not much here . . .) seem to be doing. But while I like this emphasis, I'm not sure that this doesn't tend to work as an overkill on the other side (perhaps this is necessary?), and serve to retain and reinforce the dualistic "either-or"/"us-them" categorising that we presumably want to avoid. Theoretically this should be OK, working towards a transcendence of this opposition—but I'm not sure how this happens in practice.

For the thesis I've been thinking about stylistics: how to evolve a way of writing poetry about epiphany which isn't saturated with the ideology of patriarchal / technological culture, and the implications of using metaphor here, or of not using it. And your work in the light of these questions: very interesting, and quite difficult.

Outside the window, there is white mist, and Table Mountain is disappeared behind it. It is cold and drippy, and a warm ginger kitten is nesting on my lap. I am sending you these copies of Bushman and Hottentot poems—from the *Penguin Book of South African Verse*. They may not be familiar to you, and I think you'd find them interesting.

Thank you again for your letter,

Yours,

Julia Martin

May 29, 1984 · Skipskop

Dear Gary,

I'm writing to you from a little fisherman's cottage in a little village called Skipskop, somewhere on the last bit of

Indian Ocean before Cape Agulhas, the southernmost tip of Africa. The village is tiny—about ten houses—no shops, many seagulls, many smooth white and grey stones, white sand, scrubby Cape bushes—"fynbos"—and two mice in the cottage. One of them has just come out now and is sitting watching me: fat, stripey brown mice, with rubbery tails. When the tide is low you can see the ancient fish traps, hundreds of years old. They look like this: [drawing] and were made by the Khoi people who lived here before the white men came.

These traps go all the way up the coast for miles, and because there are hardly any people about, there is no one to disturb them. But this won't last for long: although this whole area is known as the De Hoop Nature Reserve, and therefore, one would imagine, "protected," it has recently been taken over by ARMSCOR, to be used for testing and launching missiles. The mentality of these people is quite extraordinary—in this case, quite an unusual amount of public protest had no effect at all. By the end of the year, all the fishing people will have had to leave, and the cottages will be all closed down.

Driving here (four hours from Cape Town), I felt very much like your "grasshopper man in his car driving through" in one of the Songs for Gaia. I was travelling fast to get here before the storm, rain all about me, mist, headlights on at midday, the road a shining silver strip into the hills. I was aware of the very green shapes of hills, brown ploughed earth, glances of blue sky, but unable really to see them, to become a participant. One of the last towns I passed through was called Riversonderend, which means "river without end"—I remembered the scroll painting, and your use of the name.

And now, may I ask you some more questions? Your answers to my previous ones were so helpful and attentive.

About *Axe Handles:* [. . .] The section "Nets"—you must be familiar with some of the ideas involved in work on the so-called "Holographic Paradigm." My contact with it is from the collection published by Shambhala called *The Holographic Paradigm*, edited by Ken Wilber. In an article there, Marilyn Ferguson describes it as follows: "In the heaven of Indra there is said to be a network of pearls so arranged that if you look at one you see all the others reflected in it. In the same way, each object in the world is not merely itself but involves every other object, and in fact *is* every other object." This is surely the same as the "vast jewelled net" you described in *Earth House Hold,* and which I understand to be at least one of the meanings of "Nets" in *Axe Handles.* Could you tell me more about this? And about whether, and to what extent, the metaphors for reality suggested by *The Holographic Paradigm* are useful to you. Related to this is a question about your attitude towards the recent drawing of parallels between the New Physics and mystical philosophy—the sort of work that [Fritjof] Capra and others have done. Am I pushing things a bit, to read this sort of thing in your poems (e.g., in "Wave"—which is I think my favourite of your poems—the interplay of grain and wave, etc.)? Ken Wilber, also in *The Holographic Paradigm*, is very hesitant about the easy extrapolations into mysticism of this and other theories in physics, dismissing as "pop holistic philosophy" the current popularisations of the Avatamsaka Sutra—do you have any comments on this? I have been thinking a great deal about what it means to use metaphor in poetry, and so this comment in the same book caught my attention (regarding the implications of Pribram's work): "He suggested that there is no such thing as metaphor—or, in a sense, that all metaphor is true. 'Everything is isomorphic.'" Does this have any bearing on your work? What would you say to the claim that is made fairly often about your poetry, that it makes little or no use of metaphor, tending towards the metonymic pole of discourse, and therefore requiring syntax to assume greater significance than is usually the case—that is, if you wish to say anything at all to these critics, which from my point of view I hope you do. . . .

In *The Real Work*, you mention wanting to explore the mantric possibilities within English. I'm very interested in the kind of linguistic change-of-gear that happens when a poem uses mantra (as in, say, "Regarding Wave," with what seems to me to be movement from a description of Vak to an essentially nonreferential last line). But I can't imagine how this could take place in English—we don't have words or syllables that function in a linguistically comparable way . . . or did you perhaps intend something quite different?

Related to this is a rather pernickety question about the poem that appears under the title "Gaia" in *Songs for Gaia*, a slim volume which I enjoyed very much. The poem appears in *Axe Handles*, but with an alteration: the final "ah" has become "ha" . . . I'd been thinking a fair amount about bījas and the appropriateness of "AH" in relation to Vak, Gaia, etc. and so was rather taken aback to notice the change. Is this intentional (and if so, why?), or was it the fault of some typographical joker?

I'm familiar with James Lovelock's book *Gaia*—he describes "a complex entity involving the earth's biosphere, atmosphere, oceans and soil: the totality consisting of a feedback or cybernetic system which seeks an optimal physical and chemical environment for life on this planet." Does this coincide with at least some of the aspects of Gaia for you? Would it be accurate to say that to speak of Gaia implies, epistemologically, a systems view of things—as opposed to the polarising opposition of Cartesian analysis?

May 30

Next morning.

This morning there were tracks outside the cottage in the sand: as well as the usual dassie (hyrax) and small buck, it seems that a fairly big cat passed by in the night—probably a lynx or caracal—trotting down to find the fish leavings from the boats. There were also small pad prints about the size of a domestic pussy, this probably one of the small wild cats that live around here. I read yesterday that this area is the main wintering / calving place of the South African stock of the southern right whale. When the decision was made to use the place for missile testing, no ecological survey had been carried out, and the one that was carried out subsequently, because of public pressure, merely confirmed the computer's original findings that this was the best site in the country for the research.

Here are some brief questions:

- What is manzanita like, and why does it recur so often in your poems?
- (my curiosity, really) What is the origin of the last poem

in the "Little Songs for Gaia" section in *Axe Handles*—"I
am sorry I disturbed you . . . "?

- [. . .] In your letter you mentioned a discussion of Jung
  that you wrote years ago: is this generally available, and
  how could I get hold of it?

- In *The Real Work*, you mention that cities too have
  a rhythm: could you comment on this? What do you
  suggest for people for whom the option of rural life
  really isn't available?

And now these are the questions that I've left till last,
because they seem the biggest and most difficult to ask:

The Goddess—in what respects (if at all) has your sense of
the Goddess altered or developed since your early description
of her in the commentary on the Haida myth? This relates to
a larger question about the significant stylistic changes your
poetry has undergone—is there anything here you wish to
comment on? Could you expand on what you said to Paul
Geneson (interview published in *The Real Work*) about how
poetry functions to change consciousness in a society? Does
your sense of this come close to the idea that by effecting a
qualitative change in a part, a similar change is enabled to
occur in the whole?

It would be presumptuous to ask you to respond to all

these questions, but I can ask you as I did in the previous letter to comment on those you find interesting. As I write, I'm aware of how little these questions finally coincide with the profusion of those still in my head, and how much better a conversation would be. Nevertheless, I would greatly appreciate any comments you can send me. Please forgive these awful typing mistakes.

My greetings to you and your family,

Yours,

Julia Martin

p.s. About a comment of yours about *Regarding Wave* regarding the etymological intersections of energy, woman, song, and "Gone Beyond Wisdom"—could you say something more about this? I gather that you are speaking about Vak here, among other things. (I've read Woodroffe's *Garland of Letters* and some other things about this, so I think I understand what you mean here.) . . . But how does this relate to "Gone Beyond Wisdom," which I've understood to refer to "OM GATE GATE PARAGATE . . . " Where exactly does the emphasis lie in "Gone Beyond Wisdom"? Is this transcendent Wisdom, Prajnā, or transcendence, "going beyond" Wisdom? And how does this relate to your comment in your previous letter that "illusion and wisdom are one in the territory of this mystery"?

Many questions, and huge interest on my part. – JM

August 20, 1984

Dear Julia,

We are in our hot summer season here, intensely dry, keeping the garden going with daily irrigation, and enjoying rambles in the high country mountains. Also, August is a month for Zen practice in this community. Our teacher, Robert Aitken Roshi, visits for the whole month from Hawaii. I'm grabbing a few days between meditation retreats to catch up on my mail, and your long and interesting letter has come up. Let me jump right into it.

1. About "nets"—I haven't read Ken Wilber, or Marilyn Ferguson for that matter. But the metaphor of "Indra's net" is indeed what I was invoking in *Earth Household*, and it refers to the "jewelled net of Indra" described as a metaphor for mutual embracing, mutual interpenetration, complete interconnectedness, and simultaneous maintenance of unique individual existence. It is in the Avatamsaka sutra, "the jewel ornament sutra" known in China as the Hua-yen sutra, and in Japan as the Kegon-Kyo—the philosophy of Mahayana Buddhism that Zen most clearly manifests. It has been described as Buddhist phenomenalism, among other things. Thomas Cleary has translated it, and the first of three volumes is now out from Shambhala in Boulder. Francis J. Cook

has written a book on it, and there were several others. See below. The whole thing is indeed a kind of "spiritual ecology," and it is in the koans of Zen study that one actually explores it.

2. I have not followed much of the new Eastern / Western physics, Capra and all that. For all I know, they may be onto some very good things. My scientific interests run more toward biology and field ecology, and the Buddhist position is basically not that concerned with ontological models anyway. As for metaphor, the definition (and use) of metaphor can be vastly shrunk or vastly expanded. Almost all of the poems, in *Regarding Wave* respond to a subtle thematic metaphor. The same for all my other books. Metaphor is not trotted out as a short-term device section by section in poems, but amounts to subtle controlling imagery that binds whole cycles of poems together.

3. About mantra: Have you seen Sir John Woodroffe's *The Garland of Letters*? I see—looking at your letter again—that you have. That is such a nifty little book on mantra and bīja. I have not studied and thought out the mantric possibilities and lines as far as I'd like to, but sense that there is a "seed-syllable" power moving on a number of levels, in all languages, from the nonsense syllables to the archaic and persistent roots of words. (Paul

Friedrich's *Indo-European Trees* is a book on tree names and proto-Indo-European, related to the distribution of species ten thousand years ago. Turns out certain key tree names are the most persistent bījas in the Indo-European family.) I changed "Ah" into the "Ha" in the Gaia poem deliberately. I felt that the Ah syllable was too predictable and not explosive enough, not evocative enough.

4. I got the language and thought of Gaia from Jim Lovelock and Lynn Margulis. I've met Lovelock and spent some good time with him. He is amazingly sanguine about the strength of the world's biosphere to resist shock. I hope he is right. But, taking the term and the push from Lovelock was possible because I (and lots of the rest of us) have always felt that life on earth was in one sense one being. And, of course, ecosystems are systems and on one level operate by the laws of thermo-dynamics, inevitably.

And some answers to your brief questions. Manzanita is a very common West Coast summer-dry climate bush, growing from a few inches tall in some species to fourteen or eighteen feet. *Arctostaphyllus* species. It has a little red berry at the end of summer that looks like a little apple, hence the name. Perhaps the most typical understory plant of the Sierra foothills, and a common component in all types of California chaparral (and northern Mexico). Smooth red bark, tough smallish leaves that resist evaporation of moisture. The "I am Sorry I Disturbed You" poem is from a dream. And here is a list of my different publications; to go into it more than that you could obtain Catherine McNeil's *Gary Snyder Bibliography*.

I believe the discussion of Jung that I refer to is one of the chapters in my essay *He Who Hunted Birds in His Father's Village: The Dimensions of a Haida Myth*. I'll put a copy of this in the mail to you. You should maybe want to have it anyhow. (I see you've read that too.)

City rhythms: I'm not sure how to define or locate the specific periodicities of cities—especially since I imagine they are all becoming more and more similar. A city like San Francisco, which is cut off on three sides from the surrounding land by water, a peninsula, with only two bridges feeding it, has a more measured pace than a city like Dallas where traffic is converging from all directions and leaving in all directions simultaneously. A city like Kyoto, when I first went there in 1956, had very little automobile traffic, but a steady *clang clang* of old-style street cars, and a number of handcarts and even oxcarts still in the street. You can imagine what a non-fossil-fuel city where everyone is moving on horseback or on foot would be—definitely a different rhythm.

The hills or flatlands, rivers or streams, winds and clouds, all contribute to what the specific sense of the mode of any given city is. The city that I know best of all cities, where I lived longest, is Kyoto, Japan.

Now your last questions. About how my sense of the Goddess might have changed over the years. Undoubtedly when I was younger I was in the thrall of a pretty anthropomorphic goddess-archetype. That is a vision which I can still easily enough call up, walking out of the moonlight at the edge of the meadow, or out of the mists on a mountain peak. But the goddess is also a metaphor; we only divide the world up into two sets—such as essential and karmic, or noumenal and phenomenal, or wisdom and compassion, for arriving temporarily at certain kinds of clarity. But in the uncompromisingly nondualistic Buddhist view, which is an experiential view, not merely abstract and philosophical, these divisions are really just means, and the world is one. Or, as Yamada Roshi says, "not even one." There are such terms in esoteric Buddhism as the *garbha* (womb) realm and the *vajra* (thunderbolt) realm. But all of these are studied to the point of dissolving the dualism, even while maintaining a healthy understanding of the multiplicities by which things function. *Prajna paramita* is the "perfection" of a kind of wisdom that goes beyond such distinctions as being / nonbeing, yin / yang, essential / phenomenal, wise / ignorant, or even enlightened / unenlightened. The wisdom that has done this is the wisdom that has "gone beyond." All of this is blocked out somewhat clearly—at least the intention is clearly there—in the Heart Sutra. But to make the circle interesting, the esoteric Buddhist tradition represents the wisdom that goes beyond all dualisms as . . . a goddess. I find this charming. For "wisdom that has gone beyond," "illusion and wisdom both have been left behind."

But all of that is conceptual, poetical, and somewhat abstract. What is more useful is to know that these sketchy directions, which can be found in Buddhist philosophy, Zen poetry, and in some degree in my poetry, can be personally reified through the practice of zazen, a mode of study via the old Zen koans, and work with a teacher, a Roshi, brings something that seems so mysterious and remote as "gone beyond wisdom" within the reach of everyone. This is even more extraordinary. It is what our contemporary Zen study is all about. And the gate to it is the first case in the *Mumonkan* collection, a koan called "Joshu's Mu."

The Zen master Dogen, Japan, twelfth century, has written the most accessible—if you can call it that—prose along these lines, and a book of his essays in translation is coming out in its first readable English translation next spring from North Point Press, the same publisher that did *Axe Handles*.

Julia, your letters are beautiful and to the point. I feel in reading them and in responding to them that I know something of you, and obviously our minds have run along similar lines. I wish you'd tell me a little more about yourself . . . what brought you to these studies, what you are doing now, what you will be doing with them. And frankly, whatever other help I can give you in pursuing them to the point that they are intimately satisfactory to you, I'd be happy to do it. And so to stimulate a little more of a personal exchange, I'm sending along some other miscellaneous stuff that touches on our life here, some photos of me and my family, and I hope that you might be able to respond some time in kind. Your friend in the Northern Hemisphere and the Western Hemisphere away.

Gary

Thomas Cleary, *The Flower Ornament Scripture*, vol. 1 (Boulder: Shambhala, 1984)

Steve Odin, *Process Metaphysics and Hua-yen Buddhism* (Albany: SUNY Press, 1982)

Francis Cook, "The Jewel Net of Indra," in *Hua-yen Buddhism* (University Park: Pennsylvania State University Press, 1977)

June 15, 1985

Dear Gary,

The first, most important point of this letter is one brief question: may I have your permission to quote in my thesis:

1. From your comments in letters to me, and
2. The one-page biographical account that you sent me?

The thesis won't be published—only about ten copies made for friends and examiners. Perhaps you would like a copy? The reason for this abrupt request is that I've just realised that of course I must ask you, and the time for my submission of the thing is suddenly very close. I know you have mountains of correspondence, but I wonder whether you could (this once) send me the briefest "yes" or "no." A postcard would be fine. I'm sorry to ask you like this.

I wonder whether you received my last letter—photographs, etc., and news of our wedding-to-be. Here are two pictures of Michael and me during the ceremony: Midsummer's day, and people were singing, playing instruments, reading aloud—I read "Prayer for the Great Family." It was a wonderful day, and we're enjoying being married, although having lived together for some time, the difference is rather subtle.

Now it's winter, thick mist and rain, rain, rain. Cars won't start and chemist windows display boxes of tissues and remedies for colds and flu. Tomorrow is Soweto Day, June 16th, and the university where I teach has broken up for holidays for fear of what the students might get up to in commemorating the experiences of that time—now nine years ago. It is very difficult to know how to live in this country. Increasingly blatant police brutality and intimidation are terribly effective in paralysing one's sense that it is possible to do anything. Anything, that is, to change the horrible conditions which your media must now be full of. And yet leaving, emigrating, as some of our friends have done, does not seem possible. There are too many reasons for being here, in spite of (because of) the "situation."

One of these reasons is the work that I do: teaching so-called "coloured" people language and literature. The "language" (English as a second language) is obviously much needed, although our circumstances make things difficult: huge numbers, for example—1,400 [first-year] students in the English department and twelve staff members. . . . The other teaching generally involves smaller classes. In this context, the particular material that we're studying (English literature) isn't for me the most important focus. Rather, as I've said to them, I want to use our reading of texts to develop ways of working and thinking that would seem to be valuable in anything they're doing. Unfortunately, most of the students come from very inadequate school backgrounds, very authoritarian teaching methods. This means that although they will tend to be fairly well informed about radical politics, their sense of what this involves tends to be rather narrow. Many of them are burdened with incongruously conservative ideas about, say, teaching and learning, and feel somewhat uneasy about my attempts to subvert them. And then, many of them are part-time students, working long hours during the day, and coming to classes at night. The way I work with them does demand more of their own time than a formal lecture-and-note-taking situation would, and they sometimes just can't fit it in. So: these things are not easy. But they do seem to make a kind of sense.

I must now go out with hat and raincoat and boots to catch the post. Mist is now so thick that the mountain has disappeared.

Warm greetings to you all.

Julia

July 3, 1985

Dear Julia,

Your fine letter with photographs *did* arrive, and we enjoyed the surprising sense of sameness-and-difference in seeing and hearing of your life and friends. I was slow to respond, then, because kept planning to take more photos to send you, which never got taken.

Yes, you may quote from my letters etc. whatever you like. And I *would* appreciate a copy when ready.

Recently I've been spending time when possible in Berkeley with Charlene Spretnak, who edited *The Politics of Women's Spirituality*. She brings the Goddess, Green politics, Buddhism, Feminism, all together in her own work. I'll send you one of her short pieces.

Am off to Alaska with Kai (seventeen) for all of August— leading a field trip in the Brooks Range for the University of Alaska.

More anon,
Gary

March 7, 1986

Dear Julia,

Thank you for the news of yourself, the photos and news of all your country's turmoil—so much of the pain comes through—what dilemmas. And your thesis arrived, slowly, and I've read it all. It is very clear and clean and I appreciate it very much. I want to write to you in more detail later. But I am

1. Writing a prose book on culture and wilderness—for North Point Press—against a deadline—and
2. Getting ready to teach the spring quarter at UC Davis (two hours from my house—I only need to go one night a week) and I haven't taught formally in twenty years, so it takes a little planning.

What are you planning to delve into now? Do you plan to pursue some of the ideas in your thesis?—the biology of interactions—Hua-Yen and Zen studies—further poetics— what? The Goddess and her manifestations?

I guess what I'm asking, what of my own territory and interest can I further share with you, and, I'd like to know more about you and where your mind's going.

(The connection with the university—Davis is one of the main campuses of UC [the University of California], and a major biological & agricultural research center—will be helpful. Library facilities—insights into agribusiness politics—and avenues to help out worthy scholars through.)

More later. Greetings to Michael.

Yrz, Gary

January 8, 1987

Dear Julia,

I dare say you know there's pretty much a news blackout

on whatever comes from South Africa, so we know almost nothing of what is transpiring in your country these days. Your letters are all the more welcome. I am not terribly communicative the last few years because of the drive to keep up writing and research on several concurrent projects, as well as doing the work around the farmstead (and now the one-quarter-a year teaching), so if my letters seem succinct, that's why, what I'd prefer with friends & correspondents would be to hunker down in the sauna for a long talk, or over several glasses of wine.

Your writing on my work has meant more to me than I have clearly stated. Several times tears came to my eyes, as I realized that I had "gotten through" when I read your thesis. So I wish, for you and me both, we could see some of it published. One of my colleagues at UC Davis is reading it right now, as part of his project to collect and publish an anthology of essays on my work. . . . He may write and ask you if there is some part of it you'd be willing to slightly redo for essay publication here. But that's only part of it. I'd like to see more done. His name is Patrick Murphy.

I was one of the earliest members of the Buddhist Peace Fellowship . . . it is a small group to be sure, but has managed to challenge the Buddhist world (with its spirit of engagement) and the Pacifist world (with its insistence on including "all sentient beings" in the peace concern) in a few years. Joanna Macy is wonderful. So are some lesser-known people in it, Jenny Huang, a Vietnamese woman in Los Angeles, for one.

Conferences: how big, and how official, a conference would it take for your government to give you support to come to it? How much money, if any, would you need from this end? Something might just turn up.

How did your Tibetan retreat go? I have great respect and admiration for the Tibetan paths. . . . My practice has always been Zen, but much of my reading Tibetan. Zog-chen or mahamudra seem very close to Zen. I'm enclosing in this bundle a newsletter from our own home sangha, where Masa is one of the leaders & everybody is a neighbor. And a number of other little things for you.

Winter here, lots of deer out the window & millions of robins feeding on manzanita berries in the woods.

Warmly yours,

Gary

Greetings to Michael.

Julia—further news and comments.

- Since our two sons are now away to school, Masa and I have time to have real companionship and conversation (and leisure for high-quality loving) like we haven't had

for years. It is quite wonderful, this rediscovery of each
other.

- We've been reading:
    James Hillman's *The Dream and the Underworld, Inter
    Views,* and *Healing Fiction*
    Christine Downing's *The Goddess*
    Jean Shimoda Bohlen's *Goddesses in Every Woman*
    Dogen's *Moon in a Dewdrop*—a wonderful presenta-
    tion of Dogen's thoughts—best so far
    Also, Norman Waddell's translation of the Zen
    Master Bankei, called *The Unborn*

All of the local Zen group has been working between
Hillman and Dogen lately—various modes of throwing
light on our meditations and what they turn up—those long
hours—and the vocabulary of "Goddesses" as selves within
has been very useful to many women, and men too—

One of the women's groups meeting at the Honolulu
Zendo has been reading erotica written by women (the book
Pleasures by various hands), with a mind to turn the Zen eye
on women's eros—

And I'm at present working on a prose book on the wild
and the cultivated—something of an area I might end up
calling "Depth Ecology" (Jeffers's Line "Man is perhaps the
dream of Nature")—

Am thinking of periodicals.

Yrz,

Gary

March 15, 1987

Dear Gary,

Thank you very much for your letter, book, and collection of things to read. Something perhaps about the combined significance of *Upriver Downriver* and *Left Out in the Rain* meant that your package was very sodden when it arrived, legible but travel-weary, looking as though it had swum here most of the way. I was so pleased to get your book. I had written to a New York bookstore for it, but no reply. Maybe because of South Africa. The whole process of getting books from the US is very slow and expensive: it would have cost me the buying equivalent of $50! We've found the ecology material you sent inspiring and useful—one immediate result being the (enclosed) proposal Michael made for extending the focus of our antinuclear organisation to include an explicitly ecological position.

The day before your package arrived we spent a wonderful day with a young Zen teacher from California, Steven Allen. [...] Why can't we have access to people like this more regularly? Whatever one says, it surely is better to be in touch with a real live teacher? That led me to thinking about how different things are in this regard in the US, and how paradoxical that is: so many alternative (and often very impressive) visions and practices which are made possible by the very state which they oppose—AMERIKA, awash with money, triumphing on the backs of the Third World. No other country can afford to support so many glamorous alternatives. I can't quite work out what to think of that— what do you say? I'm not cynical, just confused. [. . .]

It's Sunday afternoon, blue sky and clouds, and the plants on the verandah growing green and lush after good rains yesterday. We don't have much space, but we do like to grow basil. This year we have more plants now than ever before, and several varieties. [. . .]

Julia

August 28, 1987

Dear Julia,

Almost half a year since I got your letter. I've been working or traveling in the mountains all this time, first at UC Davis, then to Alaska and the high Sierra on some thought and study ventures. Walking in the mountain wildernesses & in the depths of great cities is my meditation & angle of approach to the times right now. Prose book still underway, on wilderness & civilization. "Good, Wild, Sacred" a part of that. Alaska and China-Japan are two poles, New York City is another pole of that.

Your comment on America awash with money, on the back of the third world, supporting glamorous alternatives. Yes. In a sense. But the correction would require it to be said: the wealth in America is at the top, and there are vast numbers of very poor people, not all of them black or brown by any means. The US is not economically top country, some of those northern European places like Sweden and West Germany are higher. Even Japan, these days. Homeless visible in the streets of every city & some of the larger towns; real rural poverty, numbers of school dropouts that are never pursued, if kids quit school these days the schools forget them—lousy schools in any case. Most of the US has a kind of hard-bitten disorderly anti-intellectual anti-establishment funk. Japan, Europe, so neat and motivated by comparison! Japanese department stores full of real goodies, with taste, and their homes tasteful, good food in restaurants. Most of America is low class, low taste, funky, rough, tacky, and—funny. The humor is the saving grace. And the alternatives one hears about are made possible, in part, by that looseness and funk. The government doesn't pursue us, we can drop out of sight and be forgotten and try things out on a low budget. And some of the higher visibility alternatives are hard work, essential, struggling projects.

What I get impatient with is the "New Age" high-tech utopians with a lot of untested hippie-philosophy spiritual rhetoric still floating about, but no work with machines or the hands. Here, where I live, people work hard and are making it work, without spiritual pretentions.

Even though the Ring of Bone Zendo is clearly one of the liveliest Turtle Island Zen enclaves going, and a model for the possibility of lay Zen practice, its members don't think that way, they just do it. So, for some of us, living in the corners and margins of Babylon, we might as well be in the third world ourselves. New York, Washington, even San Francisco, so remote. And we know there are about ten thousand families who do own the wealth, the power, the nation, and have rigged the vast military machine, with the often unthinking support—marginal support in its way too—of a paradoxically libertarian / anti-Communist masses of folks who have not much changed since days of De Tocqueville.

It's weird. In my own case, of course, I've had some conventional success—have somehow supported myself in Amerika by my poetry & garden. It's partly luck; a lot of it is also hard work. And the unfolding of our little Sangha & the creative joy I get from teaching and doing Bodhisattva-

Zen with this group is probably the best thing in my life, even better than my solitary rambles on the high-country granite slabs and snowfields. Masa is a teacher in the Zen work too.

I do hope you've recovered from afflictions and infections. I'll bear in mind that it takes a *big* conference to get you over here. . . . What does big mean anyhow? . . . Maybe something will come along in the area of nature & wilderness writing / criticism / deep ecology / feminism that will be just the thing to draw you.

Thanks also for your outline of "Wild and Tame." I've been working on something similar myself. In your dichotomy I think you've failed to push far enough, far enough even into the dictionary. Here's what I mean:

Standard dictionary meanings of *wild* gives you this:

Of land: uncultivated, unpopulated.

Of plants: noncultivated, nonpropagated.

Of animals: undomesticated, untamed, also out of control, difficult.

Of individuals: unruly, resisting authority, rude, unrestrained, promiscuous, free, freedom-loving.

Of societies: resisting central authority.

Of art, of people: artless, free, spontaneous.

What can be noted here is the predominantly negative

approach. But turn the language around! What do you get when you avoid the *un-* and *non-* prefixes?

Of land: a place freely manifesting itself without human intervention.

Of plants: self-propagating, self-managing.

Of animals: self-propagating, self-managing, free.

Of individuals: a person not conforming to elite manners, self-governing, freely expressive, sexually open.

Of societies: fiercely independent, self-governing, proud.

In general, in regard to land, plants, animals, wild is a way to speak of intact & functioning natural ecological systems. A wild system is a healthy, orderly system; we are speaking of mannerly & orderly processes within the realm of wild nature; in fact anti-entropic in its process. Civilization from this perspective is disorderly and entropic. The positive definitions of "wild" lead me to see it almost identical with the Chinese term "Tao"—Chuang-tzu says, What is the difference between the human and the natural? The natural is that horses and oxen have four feet. The human is halters and nose-rings. The order implied is "out of harmony with nature" and thus disorderly.

Further on, "wild" can be said to be close to "essential nature," "original nature." "Reality."

These things are good to work on. Here are some poems

& other bits & pieces for you all. I'm writing a number of love poems too, right now . . . will show you someday.

Best to you both—

Gary

December 3, 1987

Dear Gary,

I wonder how an express letter gets delivered to Kitkitdizze? It always seems extraordinary that letters and objects can fly overseas to places where one has never travelled. But this time there's a chance that I might be able to follow. I've just had a proposal for a paper accepted for a conference in England next year. The conference will be held at Durham University and has been titled "Where the Wasteland Ends: European Literature and Theology in the Twentieth Century." But they don't seem to be sticking to "European." I will be arguing that we can't afford to see terms like "wasteland" as being metaphoric: the earth may yet become a wasteland. With this in mind, one understanding of what has been (or must be) "saved for belief" (their terms) is a sense of the preciousness of plant and rock, animals and sea, and the network of exchanges by which they are connected. I haven't written the thing yet, but I expect it will be called something like "Gary Snyder's Spiritual Ecology."

I'm telling you all this now because there's a chance that I might be able to extend this trip to include a visit to the US. My university will probably pay for the fare to England (otherwise I can't go), and it seems possible that they might give me some extra leave and fund me further if I can give good academic reasons. So I thought, what about an interview? There are so many things I'd like to talk to you about, and some of them could be formalised into an interview over a couple of days. How do you feel about this? If you like the idea, when would it be convenient? [. . .]

Another thing I've been meaning to ask you: if money etc. could be arranged from this side, would you consider visiting South Africa sometime? A friend of mine (who was an abbot at a Zen centre for some years, and is now working as an advocate!) who's known your work for some time asked me to find out. We both thought that there are many people here who would like to meet you as a teacher. Of course this is a tremendously fraught place in so many ways, but it is also very beautiful, and the fynbos ecology is fascinating and varied.

Thank you very much for your last letter and all the enclosures, particularly the poems you sent. Your comments about "Wild and Tame" were very useful. In fact I've left that particular piece as it is because I sent it months ago for the publishing deadline of that book. What you said about

America and the Third World also helped to make things seem more complex than I'd imagined.

Would you mind letting me know as soon as possible about an interview? The university machinery is ponderous and long-winded, especially when one's trying to arrange things that cost money.

My greetings to you all,

Yours,

Julia

December 27, 1987

Dear Julia,

A quick answer—so you can move on it. I'll be leaving California mid-September for a research trip to Tibet (!). If you can get here before that we can cook up some time together. Would be glad to collaborate on an interview or anything else you'd want to do.

However: UC Davis (on the quarter system) is closed then, not opening till late Sept. So I don't see how we can arrange anything official, at least on the regular academic schedule. Some off-season lecture could be scheduled—there at Davis, or our local cultural center? Let me know how it looks—

Best,

Gary

April 16, 1988

Dear Julia,

I am delighted that you will be able to come in September, that we will finally get a chance to meet and talk. The timing seems good, I will be leaving September 20th for my month in Tibet and China. Time may be a little tight during that period—a lot is happening this summer, including my own studies and preparation for the trip, but I'm sure we will be able to spend some hours and days together, & definitely a hike. [...]

I think we can be flexible about it and gear to both of our schedules. If you don't have to set it down right away, we can arrange it on the phone once you get to the Bay Area. I would imagine at least two or three days staying over here, and if it works out maybe an overnight hiking and camping trip up in the higher mountains. I won't guarantee entirely that I'll have that much free time though—we'll have to see how this preparation for Tibet goes. In any case, we will certainly get our essential work done. If you wish to send some queries and thoughts in advance, please do. As a faculty member of the UC system, I'm sure I can help arrange library privileges for you at Berkeley and Davis, if you like. I have quite a sizable archive in the special collections section at the UC Davis library; but of course Berkeley's library is much larger, and would be perhaps more convenient for you most of the time. We can meet with the Buddhist Peace Fellowship people. Or I can introduce you to them. I would love to take you with me to visit with Charlene Spretnak, whom I am very fond of, and would welcome any chance to visit her. Joanna [Macy] travels around a lot, hard to say if you will catch her. But if she is nearby, we would enjoy that as well, I am sure.

As for the Ring of Bone Zendo, I am enclosing our recently completed "brief account." It is right here on my land, the little Buddhist temple, and you will be a witness to some of its activities if you are around here for long. I am sure. Other things you'd like to do and see—people you'd like to meet—let me know. In preparation for your visit, I'll probably be sending more bundles of stuff.

As for academic boycott business, I am not sure how all that works, but I'm definitely sure that we can interpret your visit truly in a most progressive light.

Your work on my poetry is some of the most sensitive and penetrating that has been done, especially in the areas that move me most, areas moving toward the realm of the feminine in the psyche—and the feminine. So when you ask what issues I'd like to talk about, let me throw this out: only recently it has come more clear to me that although I am in a lineage (in part) of Thoreau, Muir, and Buddhist monks and teachers as well, I bring another element to it:

Eros, & the regard for the Goddess. We might try to look at that.

Warmly,
Gary

And various I hope not too tedious enclosures.
How sad I feel for your country. And for Israel / Palestine.
The National State, arrgh!

January 3, 1989

Dear Julia,

Sorry that this has taken so long. I have had to take things as they came, which meant deadlines and firewood and car-repair type priorities. We're in deep snow now, tending the fire, fixing some broken pipes, skiing a bit, and keeping at our work. [. . .]

Carole and I enjoyed your visit very much and wish it could have been longer. Things are pretty much together now, that's why I'm finally able to give writing full attention. I hope your life and work in South Africa is looking hopeful, gad, what can I say? At least you're not living in Lebanon or on the West Bank. Be well! Hello to Michael, I haven't had a chance to read his novel yet . . . after the book's done . . .

Warmly,
Gary

March 14, 1989

Dear Julia,

Clear days and frogs croaking in the pond, cool but lovely, verging on spring. And this after the hardest winter in ten years. Much snow and freezing, impassable roads, but now though cool the weather is benign. Thank you for the good letter and Michael's poems. The turmoils go on, how wrenching it must be for everyone in your hard country. I do appreciate hearing your firsthand accounts. [. . .]

Gen went to Mexico for two months in Jan–Feb and came back in great shape!

Best—

Gary

May Day, 1989

Dear Gary,

[. . .] It's good to hear that your work is proceeding so well. I wonder how the term at Davis has been going. I've just finished a lecture course on the continuity of traditional oral forms in contemporary political poetry in South Africa. We looked at how the different oppositional groupings (tribal, Africanist, proletarian) have each attempted to establish their own legitimacy with respect to inheriting the mantle of "tradition," as played out in the poetry. It's fascinating stuff.

Greetings to you all,

Love,

Julia

Dear Gary,

[. . .] You might be interested in the enclosed postcards which I designed. We've been selling them more or less at cost for people to send to supermarket managers, pharmacists, etc. (South Africa still uses CFC aerosols, which were banned in the US as early as 1980, as well as a lot of polystyrene packaging, and most people don't know anything about the dangers.) As with the pamphlet, which I think I sent last time and which is intended for disseminating information in a sort of "chain-letter" way, the idea is to encourage as many people as possible to begin taking some kind of (decentralised) action on ecological issues. So it's partly a strategic move, consciousness-raising maybe, in a context in which the word "green" is just beginning to have new connotations. The responses here have been good. I've had lots of people writing in, wanting to get more involved, and even the accredited Left is taking a little notice. [. . .]

It's really cold here now, so it's difficult to imagine you in a just-past-solstice California summer. I hope you're all flowering. . . .

With love from
Julia

March 26, 1990

Dear Gary,

I've been thinking about you and reading your work again because . . . I'm going to be taking part in the conference in Taiwan in September! The programme sounds very stimulating, and I'm trying not to be daunted by the idea of an audience of five hundred, with simultaneous translation into Chinese. I'd never imagined myself visiting that country, which for many years has been one of South Africa's few friends (although things seem to be changing pretty fast now in terms of who will speak to whom), but now that it is happening I've found out a bit about the place, and it looks as though it could be fascinating. And of course it will be good to see you again. [. . .]

Do you know yet what your presentation will involve? I'm writing my paper now because they want it very soon in order to be able to translate it (does it really take five months to turn something into Chinese?). Your comment at the end of Sherman Paul's book ("he's working on himself in these meditations more than on me") is probably true of many of us, I think. In my case, I sense a "connection" with what you're doing, so that reading your work has helped me to think through and discover many things, and to play with "interdisciplinary" material (which always seems most interesting), while keeping a foot in the territory of literary studies. I wonder how you feel about people doing this—wryly observant and a bit flattered, I imagine. I really like the "Etiquette of Freedom" essay you published in *Sierra*, which a friend sent me from San Francisco (do you perhaps have the volume no., date of the issue, etc.?) and something I've rediscovered with great delight is the poem "The Blue Sky." I imagine you'll be doing some poetry reading at the conference, so please think about including it. I think it's wonderful.

South Africa of course remains a very different world, bursting with more news headlines than the journalists or the readers can assimilate. Your news will have been telling you about the surprising things that have been happening here. But you won't have heard about how they were dancing in the street outside our house, singing and waving flags after the news that long-banned and feared organisations like the African National Congress and the SA Communist Party were now legal, and prisoners were to be released, how one man said to me, "I don't hate you—you've never done anything to me," and a group of nurses just come off duty stood in the street, laughing and laughing with disbelief and joy, how the bus driver leaned out and shouted "Viva ANC!," and all the Muslims shook hands with each other as they left the mosque. You won't have heard about how everyone in the streets where I live seemed to be smiling more, or how I came home, shut the door and cried and cried. That night a cavalcade of buses and cars a kilometre long drove all the way from Mitchell's Plain to Sea Point (crossing the boundaries from a poor "coloured" township to a rich "white" suburb) and back (flags waving, dancing in the street), hooting their hooters all the way and shouting. They woke me up both times as they came along the main road, but I was hardly sleeping very much, heart beating, eyes opening, wondering.

The next weekend Nelson Mandela was released. Just like that. Michael (who is working on a six-month contract in an ugly place a thousand miles away) was here for the weekend, and although he was already muttering anarchist words about the deification of leaders, I persuaded him that Jason [Michael's son] could hardly say to his grandchildren, learning this date in their history books, "Oh yes, we stayed at home and had a nap that afternoon." So off we went with members of our meditation group who were meeting then anyway to hear him speak, along with the rest of Cape Town. Exciting, hot, scary ... and he didn't arrive and didn't arrive. After waiting for some hours in a crowd of about fifty thousand that was beginning to feel unpredictable, we decided to go home and watch it on someone's TV. There we saw him, briefly, and we also saw the crowd of frenetic looters right where we'd been standing, crazed enthusiasts smashing shopwindows, robbing people, and being shot by the police.... Certainly this giant man has a weighty burden of mythology to live up to. So many, many people from different political persuasions are hoping he'll turn water into wine, walk on water, heal the sick, do something that will miraculously take away all the pain. Sitting in prison all those years, he has become so deeply buried in our dreams that it's difficult to know who he is. Days before he was released, I dreamt that when he was set free, I was one of the first people to meet him. [...] He said to me, "Roses are my favourite flower," and I said, "yes, they're mine too." Then I showed him my favourite rose bush, which has been sick for the last few months. He looked at it carefully, identified the red spider mite, the powdery mildew and all that was wrong with it, and told me what to do. Now what do you think of that?

And now it's late, and I must wake up early in the morning. Do send me a note about your plans for Taiwan—I hope you'll be there for more than a momentary touchdown. In the meantime, may you enjoy the new spring leaves as we enjoy the green ones turning brown.

My love to Carole and the family.

Julia

April 8, 1990
Hanamatsri (Buddha's birthday)

Dear Julia,

What a nice surprise that we'll see you in Taiwan! We'll arrive around the 20th—but will be visiting Chinese friends for several days, out in the country.

I'm doing a little essay on Zen practice and poetry. Jerome Rothenberg and his wife will also be there.

The *Sierra* piece you read is just a part of a book that will be out in August: *The Practice of the Wild* (North Point). It was the September '89 issue of *Sierra*.

Amazing news indeed from your country. Thank you for sharing some of that!

Warmly,

Gary

Carole's greetings too—

Late 1990

Dear Gary & Carole,

It was so good to see you in Taiwan. I've been writing what I call a "story-essay" about the two weeks I spent there & will send you a copy when it's done. I really like *Practice of the Wild* very much—some excellent teaching, I think. Would it be possible to send us a copy of the chants you use at Ring of Bone Zendo? We'd like that very much. And have you seen Kurosawa's new film, *Dreams*? You must.

Love to you all,
Julia

February 7, 1992

Dear Gary,

I'm sorry that I didn't reply to your note about the conference this July. It arrived in the middle of a very demanding time for me, and I wanted to write to you, but the letter got delayed until now. Anyway, we were disappointed that you won't be able to attend the conference, but understand how busy you are. Maybe some time in the future. What would it take for you and Carole to come over for a visit? A holiday even? It's a fascinating country, we could arrange for you to see things, animals, people, places, and of course you'd always be welcome to stay with us. Think about it, anyway.

So, what was so demanding about 1991? Several things, the first big one being the sudden death in England of Michael's father, Jack Cope. After Michael returned from sorting out his belongings, we held a wake for Jack in the garden. He was quite an important SA writer, connected to a great network of people, and much loved. So old comrades, fellow writers, old lovers, friends, family, young people, old people all formed a loose circle in the courtyard and remembered what he'd meant to us. Some people had written poems and others talked without a text. I read a poem which I've enclosed here. After that there was food and drink and a trip to Clifton beach where he used to live. We scattered the ashes in the sea.

After the wake Michael & I were right back into working on a conference on ecology and politics that we were involved in organising. We wrote a series of pamphlets for mass distribution (I've enclosed one of them), ran workshops, and it all turned out to be very successful, hailed by many people as "a watershed event." So far so good. After the conference, we started to deal with the highly charged human relations generated by the presence of the person we had hired as "conference organiser." The situation was complicated by the fact that our committee of voluntary activists is composed of "white" and "coloured" people, and the employee was "black African." After about three months of agonising late-night meetings, mediations, and angry words, we decided to fire the man. And now at last the show is on the road again, with new publications out, useful networking happening again, and a wiser if sadder committee in charge. The next fact sheets will be on the politics of water, air, and energy, with a regional focus on the Western Cape. We see our work in the near future as involving contact with both grassroots people and policy-makers. It's really a critical time in SA history, when a strategic intervention can be quite influential on future structures.

Another big event came in September, when my father was knocked over by a car (driven by a paraplegic without a driving licence—sort of *Monty Python* scenario). He was very badly hurt, with numerous bones broken and a head injury which put him in a coma for ten days. My mother became very vague and confused as a result of the shock, and I, the only child, was thrown (or leapt?) into quite a major role. While he was in the coma I talked to him, sang, massaged, did visualisations, breathing, and so on throughout the day. When he came out of it he remembered this, and the staff of the intensive care unit, who'd observed it all with some degree of scepticism, said his recovery was a "miracle." But that was some time ago now. He's mobile but very frail, and very gradually emerging from massive depression ("you should have let me die . . . I just want to die . . . ") The doctors are now saying that the head injury has hastened a case of Alzheimer's, and that he may have to go into a "home"—i.e., an institution. I can't tell how much of what they're saying is a function of their training in a medical paradigm that I consider quite limited (as was the case in their attitude to whether he'd wake up from the coma) and informed in this case by an attitude towards his age (sixty-eight), or whether it is "fact" which I need to accept as such. They've done a great deal for him, but it amazes me how insistently they compartmentalise the body-mind. It seems so obvious that the psychic pain, anxiety, and loss of self-confidence which the last five months have evoked are written into the way he holds his body, his attitude to food, the way he walks, and how he breathes. And yet the medics have done nothing to engage with him as anything but a head. What sort of healing can one hope for with such an approach? One day, after I'd shown him about visualising the breath entering and filling the stomach, as a way of calming and centering, he told me he'd been practising it when he felt restless: "And I've been putting a beautiful white rose there inside my stomach," he said. I said that sounded like a good idea, and then he said, "I suppose I could put roses all the way up, and different colours!" Roses? Lotuses? As you can imagine, we've all been through a great deal of pain, discovery, and transformation as a result of the accident. To put it mildly. I've often been reminded of a phrase from a poem by the SA poet Ruth Miller: "to eat pain like bread . . . " One day I'll write a story about it.

[. . .] Now it's the new year and I'm on sabbatical. I spent the first three weeks or so ordering all my files, photocopies, and books, and putting info about all these research materials onto a computer database. So now I have quite a powerful tool—access to titles via keywords—as long as I keep it up to date. I mean to spend the time reading and writing about things that keep returning to mind as questions. Here are some of them:

- *Subjectivity* has been an important issue for literary theorists, psychoanalysis, poststructuralists, who have shown that the unitary subject, the autonomous "I," exists only in the imagination. I want to write about what ecophilosophy, and particularly green Buddhism, contributes to the picture, via notions of interdependence, sunyata, the Avatamsaka sutra, etc. I think that an advantage of bringing these perspectives into theoretical discussion is their insistence on practice, experience, and engagement as a way of knowing: a way of experiencing "self-in-environment" that implies compassionate action, the bodhisattva's vow. Any comments about this? In the course of an essay, I'd like to question some of the recent interpretations of this perspective, e.g., Joanna Macy's "The Greening of the Self" in *Dharma Gaia*, where she discusses extending one's sense of self and quotes Naess in support of an idea of "extend[ing] our notions of self-interest." I think I know what she's getting at, but it sounds to me rather similar to an expanded ego project, or Dogen's self advancing to confirm the myriad things. What do you think?

- Related to this, I'd like to do something quite accessible about *sunyata* as a basis for ecopolitical engagement, relating it to ideas in current lit theory, and perhaps using a discussion about food—sacramental eating, "interbeing," the politics of food, etc.—as a basis for examples. I suppose "Song of the Taste" and your commentary on it started me on this track years ago, but other ideas have appeared along the way. Our karate teacher once said to us, "That emptiness is so full!" Can you say something about what emptiness / devoidness means for you?

- Another evocative word is *home*, because where and how, one locates "home" (psychologically, geographically, spiritually, etc.) has important consequences for the way one relates to the world. Is it home vs. the aliens? the centric idea of home as source and goal, beginning and end? "homeless" as you define it in "Blue Mountains Constantly Walking"? Have you thought further about these things since that essay?

- On the ecopolitical front, I think I'll write some responses to the flood of ecofeminist material that is now appearing (I may be teaching a course on this at the university of Utrecht in Holland later this year), but I'm also interested in *ecofascism*. Quite a useful book called *Ecology in the 20th Century: A History*, by Anna

Bramwell, alerted me to the elements of "green" philoso-
phy in Nazi politics. There are striking correspondences
between this and macho right-wing attitudes in this
country towards "the land" and wildlife conservation,
and I'd like to write about them. Are you aware of
similar tendencies in the US?

- Although I enjoy these reflections, I'm increasingly
drawn away from the kind of work that is expected of
academics, [and] towards writing with a more personal
voice. I've started writing what I call *story-essays* as
well as the more formal academic pieces. The first one,
"Just tell the truth," is enclosed. The next one I'm doing
is about issues raised by the visit to Taiwan. I wrote
the basic thing a year ago and now want to get back to
it with a bit of distance. I've also been writing poetry
and done a sung performance at a women's festival. The
experiences of the last year have reminded me that life's
too short to spend most of one's time discussing other
people's creative work.

A last question that I've been meaning to ask since I
received the Sierra Club book about you. Of course I enjoyed
reading it and looking at the pictures, and it is a beautiful trib-
ute. I recognised in most of the pieces an acknowledgement
of your role as teacher which I've often felt when considering

the impact you've had on my life. And yet there's something about it that I don't feel comfortable with. The celebration of an individual life that the book presents, adds up, it seems to me, to a form of myth-making that tends to elevate, separate, rarify the personality in what is perhaps a characteristically American way. The effect isn't to empower the reader to find his / her own way on the trail—as I think your own work often does—but rather to inscribe another hero in the text. Is this too harsh? I imagine your response would be to laugh about it all, and perhaps it isn't that important after all. Still, I'd like to hear your response.

Michael has also been writing and making things. For our wedding anniversary he wrote a long poem (made up of eighty-nine short ones) which I think is wonderful. I'd like to send it to you because the things it's concerned with—a playful-serious sense of dependent co-arising—probably won't touch a vast readership, but I think you and Carole are among the people who would enjoy it. So, may I send the poem?

And now, end of letter. What a long one. I imagine it arriving as part of your daily wad of correspondence, and hope you can reply briefly sometime. You're often in my mind, and even when I'm not thinking about your writing, I'm interested in your responses to things.

Give my warm love to Carole and to you.

June 6, 1992

Dear Julia,

A tardy response to your multifaceted letter. Gearing up for spring teaching took something of a toll on me. It is still very busy, but as soon as school work is wrapped up I have a date on the upper Colorado Plateau, so we'd best do it now.

I am very sorry to hear that Michael's father died, and very much in sympathy with your plight, and the plight of your father. It is quite obvious to me now that there is no time in life, except perhaps in childhood, when we are not intricately involved in family obligations to our children, or to our parents, not to mention siblings. It really is part of our real life, and so I keep an eye on my eighty-six-year-old mother, try to see her once a week, and hope that she does not go in to some kind of disabling deterioration. So far she is feisty and well, and takes care of herself. (My father died in a bungled surgery in the Balearic Islands back in the sixties.) These family problems (and Michael's new career) do not seem to have abated your creative and intellectual energies a bit, however.

And so I will briefly take up the questions you raised (recalling rich sets of questions you posed to me back in the days when you were doing your MA) and see what we can come up with—

On "subjectivity"—Buddhist thought contributes virtually *everything* to the discussion, since the marks of the Dharma are Suffering, Non-self, and the Path. I can only think that all the varieties of ecophilosophy and postmodernism need quit theorizing about the self and start doing zazen—leading directly into Dogen's "We study the self to forget the self. When we forget the self, we encounter all phenomenon."

With no-self, the ten thousand things are allowed to instruct us and confirm us together with them. You have to be open / empty / to let something in / to learn.

"Emptiness" is something I have learned not to talk much about, though. It is a term to be understood through practice, and used sparingly elsewhere, because it is so easily misunderstood. It could be in some cases understood as "full" and some cases as "interconnected"—

Home is a rich term that cuts both ways. Homeless, *shukke*, a "monk" in Buddhism, means one who has left the conventions of local society for the community of the Dharma, the Sangha. It can mean, then, *true* home. I am suspicious of any easy notions of cosmopolitanism, however, that would use ideas of bigness and one-ness to displace the local, to displace "home village" or "home girl." As Dogen also says, "When you find your place, practice occurs."

I am not really very impressed by worries about ecofascism

à la Bramwell, and do not think it at all a danger here. Quite the opposite: anti-ecology fascism is what's likely. If resource shortages ever cause governments to become totalitarian and dispense resources according to central planning, that's just *plain* fascism. The few right-wingers who support wildlife and conservation are usually decent people. They are actually what you'd call right-anarchists, or right-libertarians.

About Jon's book. I had very little to do with it. It will certainly help future biographers form a rounder picture, because so many points of view have been presented. Whatever myth has been made, will be, thereby, a more accurate view, I guess. And in any case, stories will be told. As for my poetry and the book, a large percentage of the people who wrote for that are not particularly literary and many don't know my poetry all that well. It speaks to my life, our lives, our times, along the Eastern Pacific / Western Turtle Island: a bit of culture history.

Whoever said myth-making and the elevation of personality was particularly American? Look at European history.

So I hope yours and Michael's life is getting more settled. Carole sends her warm regards—(and thank you for all the good material, I'll comment on that another time).

Gary

*October 3, 1992 • Paris

Dear Gary & Carole—

We found this picture of Old/Young Man Medicine
Buddha for you. Sitting here at a café, drinking morning
coffee & eating croissants, we can see Parisian autumn
leaves on the wet black street outside, & people walk-
ing dainty dogs. The dog-shit on the street comes from
Southern African beef sold for foreign exchange: wetlands
drained, ecosystems destroyed, and Africans still starving.
We're having a great time and wish you were here. The main
pretext for this visit is some seminars I'll be giving at the
University of Utrecht in Holland.

I'll send you copies of papers sometime.

Love to you both,

Julia M.

(Yves Klein described himself as "the conquistador of the Void.")

January 15, 1993

Dear Gary,

Happy New Year to you all. For us this is the time of
long summer days and sweet basil pesto on the beach in the
evenings. It's difficult to imagine the Northern winter, but I
believe that's what you're experiencing.

*Postcard: Yves Klein, blue Portrait-relief d'Arman, 1962

The letter you wrote is dated June. My apologies for not replying sooner. I think I was away in Zululand when it arrived, and then was very absorbed in writing a paper for a seminar in the Netherlands. I do value your letters, and appreciate the attention you've given to this correspondence very much. Very often a sentence has worked to resonate within me for a long time afterwards, catalysing a shift, a new way of seeing. You wrote, for example, about what I suppose would traditionally be called filial piety, that "there is no time in life, except perhaps in childhood, when we are not intricately involved in family obligations to our children, or to our parents." That observation helped me to settle with the role I find myself having to take towards my parents. It helped me realise: OK, this involvement isn't some kind of distraction or mistake, it's part of the real work; this *is* my life—there isn't another one. Once I recognised that, I felt much easier and I'm grateful to you for it.

Thank you too for the responses to my questions about home, subjectivity, etc. You'll find a conversation with some of these issues in the enclosed pieces of writing that I've been doing this year. The Jade Salamanders story could be read as a deconstruction of / companion to my essay that appeared in *Western American Literature* early this year. The Snake man essay is an experiment that I tried out on the Women's Studies seminar at Utrecht University in the Netherlands. It provoked some Buddhists to come out of the closet, and was generally well received. [...]

So far our conversations have been quite intellectual, but this has to do with practice, which now seems more important. Some questions, then, little torch-lights in the forest:

- Teacher / student. What is a Zen teacher, and what is a student? Can the relationship function long-distance without regular face-to-face contact? [...]
- Family life / practice life. Having spent some time in immersing myself in your perspective on the householder's life—changing diapers, going to meetings, etc.—I don't see practice as being exclusively to do with sitting on a zafu. Obviously. But it does occur to me that you did spend quite some time in a monastery before reengaging with Turtle Island, equipped with certain tools that most people have not acquired. Isn't this one of the koans for Western Buddhism—the translation of a primarily monastic practice into a completely different social order?
- Sangha. Our group of about ten spiritual friends who sit together once a week on a Sunday evening, and monthly for a morning, is a powerful and supportive little community that is nonhierarchic and democratic. We're not bonded to one teacher, or even one tradition, but there is trust and commitment among us and we read some of

the same books and listen to similar tapes. How much do you think a group like this can do for one another?

In all this, what I seem to be asking is: Can Zen work without a teacher around? Or at least someone who's practised intensely in a monastic context, and without a sangha that is exclusively committed to Zen practice? I sense that in this postmodern world of global communication media (which is how we got in touch with the teaching in the first place) there may be new ways of doing things, but I'm not sure what these are, and clearly there is no substitute for the neighbourhood that is local and familiar. [. . .]

Dear Gary, busy important person, I hope you have time to respond briefly to some of this.

Give my love to Carole.

Julia

March 29, 1993

Dear Julia,

A quick answer to your last letter—much work here, so I won't take time but get to a few simple points. One is that I can't say much about the relationship between a Zen teacher and a student at this distance. A teacher in Zen is not a guru but a guide and a challenge, someone to check yourself against, but it must be someone you trust. If there is no human being around that can play that role for you in a specific way, take it as the world is your teacher—and that various individuals at various times unwittingly present themselves to you as instructors and challenges. As they say, your own mind and your own life is your best teacher. About monasteries, families, and practice, one does not expect to be a PhD while living daily life—there is a requirement of some focus and training in details and specifics. I think the same can be said of Zen, that there is a need at least for three- to five-day retreat practice periodically, and really ideally a couple of years in monastic or ashram conditions where one can intensely focus on the practice and culture of Buddhism. I really see no way around that. We don't have to invoke a monastic practice, but do have to imagine some kind of communitarian practice in which the interaction of people sharing the same goals with the same discipline is part of the training. Your ten spiritual friends sangha group is quite powerful, I'm sure, especially if it grounds itself not only in the spiritual but in the material. Sitting together, discussing dharma points together, and also getting out in the watershed a bit together and sharing your energy with the human and natural community around you, being committed to your place to some extent, is also (I think) part of our new way of practice.

One can practice Buddhism in a broad way and possibly even Zen in a broad way without connection to traditional teachers, anywhere in the world, but the style and actual accomplishments and teachings that are within something like Rinzai tradition require direct contact at some point with someone trained in that tradition. No way around that. And the more accessible Soto-style teachings at this point in our cultural history are also so remote to Occidental mindsets and so easily translated into dualistic habits of mind, or needless intellectualism, that even there I think it would be a long time before good understanding can usually be arrived at without some checking against people trained in a tradition more directly. (More directly doesn't necessarily mean having been to Japan.)

My son Kai is up in Zambia right now working at wildlife habitat mapping in the Luangwa Preserve. His address in Box 82, Mfuwe, Zambia, if you have any words of wisdom about Africa to write to him. We've heard from him several times and he seems to be doing excellently well, though a bit in shock in regard to the poverty of the area.

Hope you are all well and better—we've had enough rain for once this season.

Warmly,

Gary

p.s. Thanks for "The Snakeperson," and the ecology papers. I'll have to get to those later.

p.p.s. "Travelling to the Capital" most echoes Yeats's poem "Byzantium"—but you were on the right track.

May 7, 1993

Dear Gary,

Thank you very much indeed for your letter in response to my questions about practice. Your perspective is certainly helpful, & I do appreciate your response, when I know (or sense) how busy you are. [. . .]

I've felt much quieter, but the stormy passions of this country have been raging madly. Since Chris Hani died, people seem to have become increasingly polarised, the newspapers full of talk of civil war & masses on the "right" and the "left" using exactly the same language of hatred, fear, and death. I've been reminded often of Thày [Thich Nhat Hanh] and the definitions of practice that emerged from the Vietnam experience. In these times, his reminders that "if you want to work for peace, you have to be peaceful," and his emphasis on breathing, smiling, calmness, etc. are especially useful.

I'm enclosing the report of a march our university organised. It took place two days after a march in the centre of Cape Town which had ended in mob violence, looting, burning, chaos. . . . Now our students wanted to march to Bellville (the city nearest the university) and present a statement at the police station. Bellville is a pretty conservative place, & we'd heard that shopkeepers had hired armed guards to shoot (with live ammunition) anyone who touched their property. While the students worked themselves up into a death-defying collective mind through chanting, singing, dancing, & passionate rhetoric, we were given instructions: display calm, keep the students disciplined & peaceful, see that the group stays together, etc. We were quite frightened. It was quite possible that even if the students were peaceful (which seemed uncertain), a member of the police, or the right-wing residents, might shoot and start it all off. People were saying things like "It's like the old days—you don't know when you set out whether you're going to come back alive," "People are going to die today . . . " The students looked so young, too young to know that they're mortal, & I felt a great sense of tenderness and poignancy. What was quite clear to me, though, was that we had to go through with it. If our presence could do anything to safeguard these students, then we had to be there. So we set off, the Heart Sutra walking in my feet, hands holding other hands—a human chain of staff & student marshalls holding the edges of the crowd. As you see from the report it turned out to be miraculously peaceful, although it wasn't until we reached the university gates, two and a half hours later, that I felt able to stop being a vigilant sheepdog. We felt it was quite a victory, & certainly a heart-warming experience for us all. Why does it take such moments of *extremis* for people to walk together, holding one another's hands?

I hope you're well & enjoying the spring. I've written to Kai, inviting him to come and stay if he visits SA.

Love to Carole & to you,

from Julia

February 20, 1994

Dear Julia,

I'm finally studying up on Africa. Have been reading Bessie Head, Kofi Awoonor—am just beginning to get the picture of how complex the life of South Africa has been this past century—and I will be visiting Kai in Botswana & Zimbabwe all of April. Gen's coming too; but Carole can't come, she has to be with Kyung-jin. This trip is—in part—for finishing up *Mountains and Rivers Without End* this year. I'll fly in & out of Johannesburg—but have no plans to stop there, at least this trip. Now that I'm getting focused, though (and *Mountains and Rivers* will get done), I'd be interested in a trip to SA if another lecture possibility arises later on.

How are you & Michael? More travels, or publications? Have done three new *Mountains and Rivers* sections; more to come.

Yrz, Gary

Any other reading you'd recommend?

March 14, 1994

Dear Julia,

I'm going to try to fax this to you, and if it doesn't work why then I'll send it by mail. It was good to be mutually in touch with you, and magical to see your letter come through the machine. I am sorry to hear that your karate master has died. I hope you and your friends will be able to keep your sangha / community going with mutual teaching energies from within, and also be able to find new experts, new leaders, for the specialized things you wish to do.

After some thought, it's pretty clear to me that Gen and I will not be able to take more time on the way back to the States to visit South Africa. Your generous invitation is really welcome, but four weeks is all that either of us can spare at the moment. As you know, I'm still working on *Mountains and Rivers*, and must get right back on to that; also I can't leave Carole totally running the place and taking care of KJ by herself for much longer. It is true that to see your country just at the time of the elections would be of great interest (and some trepidation—I wish you well!) but I'll have to pass on it.

If things go well, there is a strong possibility farther down the road—a year later? not till after June '95 or later depending on my progress—that I would be available for a trip to South Africa if such an opportunity arose.

And thanks for the reading list. I am finally starting to read Michael's book! There is a bundle of some of my recent work coming by mail, some of it for the poems; some leading toward another volume of small prose pieces.

Yrz faithfully,

Gary

July 1, 1994

Dear Julia,

Well, so much to say about our trip there, in briefest of brief, after a few days we went out in the bush, the wild savannas of grass and mopane / acacia / fig tree—in two days I saw more species of mammals than I'd seen in my entire life before. Elephants drinking water, impalas running and bounding, baboons eating figs—and more and more. Steered our old borrowed Land Cruiser over a network of dirt tracks in the night by watching the Southern Cross. Went north to stand in the spray of Victoria Falls on the Zambezi, and down into the arid savanna of the Kalahari to meet with Bushmen. Kai will maybe do some maps for a newly formed San political group based in Ghanzi, Botswana, called "First People."

Hitchhiked east into Zimbabwe and visited very old cave

paintings by old-time San, including a marvelous rhinoceros petroglyph. Saw endangered rhino shit but no rhinoceros in the flesh in Matopos National Park.

Drank hippopotamus river water but nobody got sick. Flew back home the day after Nelson Mandela was announced the winner of the South African elections, people everywhere so jubilant. Our 747 out of Johannesburg was full of black Americans returning from the election. In all it was a great trip. About it, much more later. [. . .]

I wonder how South Africa is doing, we don't hear so much news about it all now, but for a while it was top coverage in all the papers . . .

Mountains and Rivers work is loping along . . .

Carole sz hello, warm hug from us both . . .

Gary

October 24, 1994

Dear Julia,

Thanks for your letter of the spring (autumn) equinox. You may indeed hope to see some rhino-shit-on-the-trail poetry. Now that I know how to see the signs, I need to figure out the grammar. The grammar of scats . . .

Maybe you can help me: I saw a book at Paul Sheller's house in Maun by Louis Liebenberg. *The Art of Tracking: The Origin of Science*, David Philip Publishers, 208 Werdmuller

Center, Claremont, 7700, South Africa. 1990. I just glanced
at this, and it was very provocative. Now I wish I could get a
copy—I wrote the publisher and they told me it's out of print.
So if you happen to run across one anywhere, or know of a
used book specialist that might have an edition available,
I would be happy to pay good dollars for it. The poem I'm
working on is actually about the "procession of animals"
right off the 15,000-year-old rock paintings in Matopos and
down the dirt track in front of the truck. And a lot of that
procession is scats and tracks.

And thanks for the work you've done on helping me get
over there, no sweat if nothing has taken shape yet. In this
light, however, I'm going to go ahead and agree with a friend
from New Mexico to go with him to Nepal for a hike up
the Khumbu Valley a year from now in October. It will be a
chance for Carole to walk in the Himalayas for the first time.
And I'll hold January / February / early March of 1996 open
for a possible venture to South Africa (or even later some
other time). Also I do agree with you, that for the time I
would be there, I should stay in the west as you suggest and
not try to crowd too much in. Eastern Bushveld.

The bioregional project and South Africa: I used to think
that this particular exercise was of use mainly to people like
Americans and Australians (and South Africans) who had
large populations of people from elsewhere, particularly

from developed nations, who are in the process of trying to become at home and responsible to the new place. Most of our bioregional talk has been framed from that standpoint. After our trip to Spain in '92, and many conversations there, I realize that there was a work that could be done with equal relevance in the Old World, and I also see that as true now for almost all of the Far East. In Spain I realized that although everyone had lived there for great spans of time, they had lost the memory of the place. They had even lost the sense of its lineaments on the ground in the present—no longer knew the lay of the land. So when asked (innocently enough) by me, "What do you suppose the original forest cover around Barcelona was before the Carthaginian logging?" I drew totally blank stares. It was not a question that anybody ever asked themselves. And the whole range of environmental history was hard to dig out, although a few people were able to talk about the effect of corporate sheep ventures all across Spain in the sixteenth (?) century, which had a very destructive effect on the landscape (not to mention the peasant society). In the same way there is a group in Italy that has been in touch with me now, who are proposing a bioregional outlook, and a kind of platform for Italy. In the case of Italy—with its perpetually faltering central government—I can see that it provides potentially non-nationalistic or racist regional community/political jurisdiction that might well work, and suits the anarchist Italian heart. Catalonian regionalism resonates to the same thing, I do believe. And in the most basic terms, a membership in place is an essential component in the matter of developing identities in multiracial and culturally diverse societies that need a ground to stand on both literally and philosophically, a place they can all come together on. I was moved to hear Nelson Mandela's speech of acceptance rebroadcast on American Public Radio when I got back to the States, in which he spoke of his perpetual memory of the Transkei where he grew up, and its green landscape, and how that was forever part of him. If, in North America, the Native Americans will grant white people, Asian people, black people, the right to be in love with the land, then—as much as the newcomers must grant the indigenous people the dignity and the respect coming to them—we have a start.

And then there are a lot of interesting educational and practical details about community economics and regional sustainability, subjects on which a lot of writing is beginning to be done right now. So, I'm including a few things here in this envelope that you may have seen already—or maybe not. And I'll see to it that further articles and books that are developing these ideas get your way.

Because I do think that there is something in it for the South African's situation, ways to form new community agreements, new political identities, that everyone can agree on, for example. And there is of course a spiritual component underneath it that is really quite profound. Dogen's "When you find your place, practice begins."

Incidentally, I was really struck by the high quality bird / tree / various natural history books, tracking books, eco-system publications done by white South Africans on the matter of Southern African nature. A lot of that is out of colonialism and imperialism, perhaps, but I see real knowl-edge and real love in it as well. That makes me hopeful. The quality of publishing and illustration is very high!

So, although bioregional practice is locally specific, the processes are similar everywhere, the approach, knowledge, and inhabitation is certainly reproducible.

Dzogchen is indeed a lot like Zen (Mahamudra is another name for the same school) and there are theories that it was a branch of Buddhism that was brought into Tibet from China rather than India. Yogi Chen of Kalimpong has written some little booklets to that point. Chan took another tack after the eighth century, however, when the kung-an, koan, system really developed and became the main teaching vehicle. Also, Chan was apparently unique in developing the custom of group meditation.

I have not heard a peep out of Tarthang Tulku's group at all lately. And here, we are moving into winter ever so imperceptibly—but I do realize I must get out and get firewood.

Love to you all—
Gary

January 10, 1995

Dear Gary,

Thanks for the excellent package of things you sent me a while ago. I've lent the book on ecological planning to a wonderful friend who's working on utopian / real alternatives for Cape Town, "the Mother City," as it's often called. And I really like your piece in *Inquiring Mind*. Michael and I read it for a day-long focus on Buddhism and ecology that we did recently.

I managed this morning to get hold of Louis Liebenberg's book for you. He's a friend we haven't seen for some time because he's been living in Johannesburg, but he's been home in Cape Town for Christmas and had some copies with him. I was pleased that you wanted the book. It's not had much attention here yet, although Harvard University Press is now interested in publishing it. We worked with Louis some years ago in the Cape Town Ecology Group. Now he's an environmental consultant doing good work on environmental policy, land rights, community wildlife management, etc. Definitely someone for you to meet when you visit. He's a fascinating, quirky, dedicated, and enormously knowledgeable person, with great stories about wild adventures. He told me that the guy on the cover of the book risked his life to save him—they'd been exhaustion-hunting a kudu in the midday Kalahari sun for an hour and a half, following the tracks, running in kudu-mind trance until they caught it. Only when he stopped at the kill did he realise that he'd stopped sweating and could hardly stand up: no more sweat left, and no water anywhere. Next thing, he knew, the brain starts boiling. So the other guy, pretty exhausted himself, ran back to the settlement for water, and his father brought it to him. [. . .]

At the end of last year I was really exhausted, and my hands got bad eczema, which literally prevented me from "doing" anything. Now, with a new year beginning (and our academic year starts in February), I mean to discover how to work in this competitive, cerebral, head-heavy university environment without becoming infused with its often very unliberating values. *Not two*, I guess—not university vs me—and yet . . . it's not easy. I feel tired of commenting on, analysing, and facilitating other people's creativity, and need to claim time and space for writing and making my own stories and sculptures. Do you have any suggestions? You kept out of it a long time, I suppose until you could work with the institution on your own terms. (Which reminds me: the program at UC Davis looks very useful. Does it ever allow for short-term involvements, i.e., from someone like me, both learning and teaching? I've been developing courses in that sort of field here, which you might find interesting.)

It's hot here, and time for a swim in the sea. The Atlantic side is much colder than the one with the Indian Ocean current, but the beaches are beautiful and you can watch the sun set. So that's where I'm going.

With love to you all—

Julia

January 30, 1995

Dear Julia,

What a wonderful surprise to find Louis Liebenberg's book *On Tracking: The Origins of Science* in your package. I had thought of asking you to look into it as a really long shot, since it was said to be out of print and here you are—close to the source. It's a wonderful gift (signed by Liebenberg to me, charming!). I hope to be able to meet him when I get over there, and to reciprocate.

All the other materials as well . . . Michael's interconnectedness, Julia's interbeing . . . &c., thank you very much. The Dharma is *radical,* when you talk about applying it in real life.

And Julia, I hope you're feeling better, yikes, eczema on

the hands. As for me, being on 50 percent time makes a huge difference. I can live *other* lives as well as the teacher's life. Of course I only get a 50 percent salary as well, which makes it a real choice. My writings, no matter how well they sell, come nowhere near making up that other 50 percent. I simply opted to have less, period. Working with other people's creativity, helping it move, I try to make into a way of learning about creativity, including my own, actually it's a lot like teaching zazen and Zen in general, you deepen yourself as you teach, as much as you know. Ideally.

And we'll see how it goes with the USIS [United States Information Service]. I'm OK not to travel next winter, too, & deferring the possibility along the line. . . . I'll have a lot of catching up to do around the place, work & projects that were neglected while finishing *Mountains and Rivers* over the last few years (which will be done soon).

Nature and Culture program at Davis is still young and struggling. It doesn't offer any graduate degrees yet, and the embattled UC system has no budget for giving us new space, a room, a secretary, or anything. We have to scrape by still. But on the chance that the possibilities of a slot for an occasional visiting scholar open up (and I trust they will eventually), send me information on courses you've been teaching that might fit into such a program.

Carole is getting ready to be active in the spring bird

migration banding & data-gathering project that our watershed group has joined in on. She did it last year and became a pretty good ornithologist. This year she'll be doing it twenty or more hours every week. It turns out our region here is a major migratory songbird nesting area (these guys winter in Central America). All through the manzanita brush and up in the pine trees. She says warm hellos—& hello to Michael—

Please note I'm on email now, address at the top, if you are using that. It's most convenient and saves time & money. . . .

Warmly,

Gary

What's a *kloof*? Western Cape looks lovely!
We do have a video monitor that plays VHF—

July 17, 1995

Dear Julia,

Summer in England, winter I guess in Cape Town. Nice to hear a note from you.

We've gone through a record-breaking wet and cool winter and spring, and even our July temperatures are a bit low. Finished with spring teaching, and trying to get back to final revisions on *Mountains and Rivers*. Schedules are beginning to bunch up over December–January–February, and with the absolute deadline on the *Mountains and Rivers* manuscript being right around mid-February, I'd like to suggest that the visit to South Africa, potentially, be moved up to 1996 [he means 1997]. With a new officer just in, that might be more comfortable for them too. If, however, this is a big problem and suddenly early 1995 is the only opportunity, the window of time that I have now is between February 12th and the 8th or 9th of March. I would rather use that time to be writing. But I do hope a visit to Cape Town will work out.

Since I don't know when I'm going to get to editing it, if ever, I thought you might enjoy taking a look at this account of my visit to Southern Africa last year. It was powerful for me, and not the end of my connection and perhaps just the beginning of a connection with Africa. If you get a chance to look at it, I'd be curious to know how you, as an African, see my seeing of Africa. . . .

I hope things with Michael, your family, and friends are going well. I'm a bit dismayed by the direction American Buddhism seems to be heading, with less and less sense of the archetypal, the mythic, and the "religious"—and less attention to the actual history of the Buddhist tradition—as it goes toward therapy and a kind of watered-down reflection of liberal Protestantism. I suppose that was inevitable . . . otherwise, as in most of the rest of the world, we look at the directions of the powers that be with dismay. In fact your country at the moment is one of the few rays of relative sanity in the current turbulence. Carole sends her regards, and my best to you and Michael—

Yrz faithfully,

Gary

August 14, 1995

Dear Gary,

[...] I have enjoyed reading your account of Botswana & Zimbabwe. You ask how do I, as an African, see your seeing of Africa? At first sight, the world of wildlife Africa that you describe isn't something I know very well. Growing up in the high apartheid era, the meaning of "game reserve" and "conservation" seemed inextricable from the culture of those white South Africans in khaki shorts, with their *braaivleis* and beer cans, and their holidays in the Kruger Park. The Kruger *National* Park, something of a state icon. So in rejecting the ideology, we didn't feel at home in the version of "Africa" it had appropriated either. But of course it isn't as simple as that. We did visit game reserves, watch numerous wildlife films at school, and one of my earliest books was *Animals of the Kruger Park*. I still have it, and the battered old watercolour paintings of the hippo, the bat-eared fox, and all the others are still gateways for the powerful, loved, terrifying beings I knew as a child. From this point of view, "wildlife" was the assumed background of our lives, a sort of given. And your stories evoke a pleasant sense of familiarity with that, and with the details of human culture that you describe, as well as something new.

So much for that. Perhaps you'd like some specific comments / questions.

(page) 1: Did you actually fly over Cape Town? Any other impressions?

5–6: I like your attention to the baboons. We see them quite often in the Cape, and they are just like that. But perhaps it takes an "outside," travelling eye to *see* them, or any of the other animals you write about, so clearly. For us it may be more difficult, laden as they are with so many stories. This calls to mind the necklace Michael has been commissioned to make: giraffes, warthogs, impalas, crocodiles, etc., all carved in wax, to be cast in gold. The issues are similar: how to make naturalistic animals that don't look like curio shop kitsch, like all the images of wild animals that prevent us from really seeing them.

7: Didn't you get ticks, wearing shorts in high grass? We'd always wear trousers and tuck them into boots.

16: Hippos. On Lake Malawi we were told that hippos kill more people than crocodiles do. "The hippo, she won't believe you," said the man who took us out in a dugout canoe, explaining that hippos don't trust your good intentions, and will often overturn the dugout and bite you. Certainly the stuffed hippo at the entrance to the Natal Museum, with its great pink-painted open jaws, was for me the most exquisitely frightening creature in the place.

17: Interesting to read about South Africans' "apprehension" regarding the elections. I suppose everyone was a bit apprehensive, but about different possibilities—white right-wing violence? marauding hordes of blacks? Now that all seems so long ago.

19: Lions. I like your description. Michael, who grew up just outside the Kruger Park, has watched lions mating. They do it on and off for days—a single session could last throughout the daylight hours, with little breaks, and a growling love song accompanying the whole transaction. We have wonderful slides his mother took of them—and of many other animals too.

21: How did you actually do the writing ("looking through the hatch," etc.)? Did you write in a notebook and transcribe it when you came home?

23: Expand on this idea of virtual indigeneity.

24: Elephants! I love this story of the ransacked camp.

When Michael was a child, they were charged by a trumpeting bull elephant. His mother put the car into reverse and told the children not to look as their guest, a middle-aged woman, peed from terror into a coke bottle. They got away, of course, but every year, wrecks were towed into town: cars squashed down to about half a metre high, with the occupants inside. People would throw things at an elephant or somehow annoy it, and the elephant would respond by sitting on the car, standing on it, and bashing it until it was flattened.

26: Oh, yes, I agree about the Jouberts' *Lions and Hyenas* video: nasty Manichean sort of America-vs-Saddam-Hussein discourse, although the actual footage of the animals is wonderful. It's been quite popular, and quite widely marketed for tourists, so is an interesting text if one's looking at media representations of wild animals. We watch it as part of my environmental literacy course.

27: " . . . actually quite charming in a middle-class Australian or white South African sort of way." My first reaction is to feel a bit annoyed / patronised by remarks like these (there are others like this). But then I might make similar generalisations myself, using "white" to indicate an ideological orientation, just as you might write about "Americans." I suppose too that from your point of view there are obvious similarities between white Australians and white South Africans. What's the problem then? Perhaps the difference is that if you (i.e., a non-South African) make this sort of statement without much context of explanation, the simplest interpretation is that it's about a category of people defined according to skin colour. That would automatically include everyone who, in spite of pigmentation, resists that sort of categorisation. So . . . how about "colonial"? Another thought: would you write in that way about black culture? (I wonder if you've heard Laurie Anderson's recent recording of her own ethnographic stories, *The Ugly One with the Jewels*. It's darkly funny and powerful, but never cynical or nihilistic. I think you and Carole would enjoy it.)

27: *Sadza*. In Natal, where I grew up, we called it *putu*, wonderful white stuff spooned from a big pot, slightly burned at the bottom, fragrant with memories of Eslina, the black woman who was my parents' domestic worker: her frightening stories, her big lap, the warm skin of her arms.

28: "black men, dressed in starched white": Zimbabwe has apparently maintained much more of the colonial forms (with the starched servitude that made them possible) than you'll find in South Africa.

29: About the necklace you bought. Michael says that

the only tradition of metal jewellery making in South Africa / Botswana was at Mapongubwe (Northern Transvaal) and died in around 900 AD. The pewter / amber object must be from North Africa, or maybe you were had.

30–31: Vic Falls and the rainbow and the little girl are wonderful, a really beautiful description.

39: Provita biscuits, etc. I like the detailed accounts of what you ate. Provitas, like the boxed fruit juices and many of the foods you mention, are basic and ordinary for us, so it's good to find them defamiliarised and revived in your words.

36: Kudu in the headlights. They often do this, often causing nasty accidents. In some parts of the country you'll see road signs showing a jumping kudu, and people are experimenting with attaching very high-pitched whistles to their cars which will scare the kudus off the road.

37–38: In the spring the male weaver bird makes a nest as part of courtship. If she likes him enough, the female will inspect it. If the nest isn't good enough, he has to start again. So you'll see many half-finished or abandoned nests that have never been used. They work incredibly fast, in quite a manic-seeming state, lots of birds all building their nests in the same tree at once.

Did you actually see any of the birds? They're wonderful bright, golden, noisy creatures.

39: Yes, precisely: children who are "not naked but not in clothing either exactly."

39: Tuelo: what does he talk about?

42: First people, firstness. I like this—are you going to develop it?

48–49: Rhinoceros painting / writing about rhinoceros-painting / writing about rhinoceros, elephant, lion. . . . Your five-point story of the art of representation reminds me of the sense I had of our karate master who died last year. When he did *kata*, our ritual form, the individual (named Jack Mathews) who was doing it became transparent to *IT*, the perfect flowing of the *kata* itself. And yet this manifesting of the *kata* was exquisitely his own, precisely his. As he once said to us about something else, "That emptiness is so full!"

52: Mandela's speech—anything more about this?

53: Bessie Head. A few years ago someone from Natal wrote a paper suggesting that she had contact with Buddhism, and I hear that there's a thesis being written on something similar. Interesting—writing against the grain of the usual readings.

54: Yes, I know what you mean. But how does one avoid this (Wallace Stevens—"the evading metaphor")? Isn't it what happens whenever we tell stories? Maybe not—rope and snake—some people *do* show us the difference.

Well that's enough, more than enough. I very much like the (sometimes meticulous, funny, charming) attention to things, and do hope you publish it in some form. [. . .]

I was interested in your comments about Buddhism in America—a point of view which I think I share. What sorts of intervention, if any, do you think could influence this? I wonder how you find *Tricycle*? It seems to me to provide a useful forum for fairly diverse perspectives, although from our situation here the flavour certainly is very North American. A new book that I think you and Carole would like if you haven't seen it already: Anne Klein, *Meeting the Great Bliss Queen: Buddhists, Feminists and the Art of the Self*. I think it's really well written, and manages very well to bring different discourses into conversation. In my own writing, I've found doing this quite difficult—the languages of theory and academic analysis, of Buddhist teaching or of personal narrative, all contribute to what I've been doing, but they do work according to different rules or assumptions. [. . .]

I hope you're well, and give my love to Carole.

Julia

August 18, 1995

Dear Gary,
Does this work?
Julia

August 19, 1995

Dear Julia,

Why sure, these things work like, as they say, gang-busters. It keeps you up with friends all over the world, & you don't even have to know (and sometimes can't know) where they are, even! They're in the space called "cyber." I haven't sorted out my feelings about email, but I do know it is intimate, easy, informal, & serves to keep people in touch. And if one likes paper, hard copy, you can simply print out the letters you want to keep. I do it all the time, & delete the others. So thanks for writing, and let's work on 1997. I look forward to your comments on my journal note on Africa. . . . Kai is moving to Portland to be with his girlfriend and work further on GIS mapping in conservation applications, Gen is working locally at carpentry & study, and living down the hill in a little cabin. Carole is working on an oral history of her family & their life in California agriculture . . . & sends her love—be well—Gary

*Julia's first email to anyone

October 6, 1995
Subject: USIS et al

Dear Gary,

I've at last managed to get a response from the local USIS person about your visit, and this is what she said: "This hasn't been appearing in the papers lately, but the US Government is having a funding crisis, which might cause it to fall. So we don't know anything about local projects at this stage. I hope you understand how frustrating this is to us." Now isn't that a rather odd thing to say? Whatever's actually going on with them, it means that we'll obviously need to stay with planning for you to come here in 1997 rather than '96. It possibly also means that there won't be any money at all, and that we'll have to look elsewhere for funding. Do you have any ideas? Is Amerika falling?

The swallows have returned from the North, and the days are longer, warmer. Jason is writing matric (the last school exams ever), and Michael and I find ourselves saying all the boring things that parents say in order to try and make their young do some work. Next year he's flying off into the world. It's strange to realise this.

This comes with love to you all from me here, typed on the blue screen of the English Department computer. No email yet at home.

With love,

Julia

November 30, 1995
Subject: Re: USIS et al

Dear Julia,

Back from four weeks in Nepal & two weeks on the East Coast. We are still not quite returned to ourselves, fall work (firewood, prescribed burns on the public land to be monitored, some readings to do) and feeling scoured and raw from the intensity of Nepal.

Yes, the government did fail for about five days, as doubtless you heard. I had been invited to read at the Library of Congress—by the new Poet Laureate, Robert Hass—and my reading was canceled thereby . . .

I much appreciated your many comments on my Southern Africa Journal. I'll respond to that when I get further caught up . . . whenever that will be. It is of course totally unedited at this point, and I haven't put any thought into publishing it. Between solstice and equinox I'll be doing the truly final work on the MS of *Mountains and Rivers*, for publication, and after that's out and has been accompanied into the world with readings & some talks, I'll take the time to reconsider what's involved with writing and publishing. It's an odd world.

We flew Bangkok to Kathmandu, my first visit there in thirty-four years. It was a medieval city then, with almost no cars. It is still magical & full of architecture and art . . . from there eastward (by helicopter) into the lower region of

the Sherpa people, the Khumbu, the area of watersheds com-
ing down from Mt. Everest (Sagarmatha / Chomolungma),
and tiny villages on remote knees, benches, & knolls with
ice fields above and canyons below. The Khumbu region of
Nepal is the highest complex of mountains in the world.
Three weeks of walking, one week above 16,000 feet, several
days going over 18,000. The noble calm and hairy energy
of yaks. The remarkable Sherpa people and their remote
and difficult life in the village, and their very warm and
living style of Tibetan Buddhism. My twelve-year-old step-
daughter, Robin, fearless among the yaks and on the rocks,
not minding the incredibly plain diet, or the "inconveniences."
Carole transcendent in the cirques of great walls of rock and
ice. Up the Imja drainage side toward Island Peak, over a
steep pass, and down to the Khumbu Glacier, & ultimately
to the ridge above the base camp of Sagarmatha. Back down
the long glacial valley past a perched meadow of stone cairn
chorten monuments to people of all lands who had died in
climbing accidents, and again into heroic villages. Listening
every day to rapid, abstract, super-intellectual conversations
between mountaineer / businessman / old Buddhist friend
David Padwa and Stuart Kauffman (biologist, author of *The
Origins of Order*), me occasionally joining in. Mostly enjoy-
ing the silence of walking as a meditation.

A full day's trail high on a steep ridge above canyons, edging past wild goats "Tahr." And then learning that the deity of Sagarmatha is a ferocious goddess of mountains (and the guardian of Lhasa) who gambles with pestilence and pain for the sake of the world. Back down to 11,500' near Namche Bazaar, the Sherpa main town, and back to Kathmandu. Some good explorations, back in Kathmandu—to the Buddhist world, & finding that active Tantric religious practice of the most explicit sort is alive and well in Nepal. The teeming truly multicultural streets and lanes of Kathmandu—

And the area we were walking was where the extraordinary snowstorm & avalanches killed sixty or so people just three weeks later, stranded five hundred.

Who knows what the USIS, or America, will be capable of by 1997. I like the term "situatedness." And I will be mostly around the rest of the winter so able to respond more briskly. You are in summer! I just read a lovely book: Miriam Shaw's *Passionate Enlightenment: Women in Tantric Buddhism* (Princeton University Press, 1994). Turns out women are empowered and often the main teachers in that tradition, which is wonderful news. Makes me want to renew my old Tantric Vows. Love, Gary

January 5, 1996

Dear Julia:

Solstice in the Northern Hemisphere, we're going one way

and you guys are going the other way. Here's my new little prose book, the last third is recent stuff, the earlier material you may well be pretty much acquainted with. Wanted you to have it. I've been out to Nepal and back—can't remember if I wrote you since then—and then involved in giving readings from the new book up and down the coast, so finally only now in January am beginning to feel really like I'm back at home again, catching up on chores. The other book here is a gift for you, *Passionate Enlightenment*, clearing up I think some of the confusion that Tantric Buddhist practice has labored under, in regard to the role women played in it. I find Miriam Shaw's thesis—that women were powerful leaders and instructors in this tradition—really exciting, and it rings true to my intuition. While in Nepal, spent some time with Buddhist scholar and thirty-year Kathmandu resident Keith Dowman, who said that the Tantric circles and their strong women's leadership still are alive and well, particularly in Nepal, but in some parts of north India and possibly Kashmir as well as in the less impacted Tibetan zones—Ladakh. Miriam Shaw studied some months with a teacher in Ladakh. I'm still in the last phase of manuscript work with *Mountains and Rivers*, but that should be done within another month or two, and it will be out in the world as a book in the fall. In June, Carole and I are joining a trip with Clayton Eshleman of Eastern Michigan University to go study caves in southern France. The new cave—just found there—has a picture of a hyena in it from 20,000 years ago. I have another poem (or prose) essay in mind, which will be about the wildlife processions of southern Africa, the processions of painted animals in the Matopos caves, the processions of animals in the archaic caves of Europe, and the circumambulations of pilgrims around mountains, particularly in Asia. Won't that be fun?

Happy new year to you and Michael. I have other things I'll discuss with you when I can get to it, the current state of ecofeminism and my Africa journals. I hope things are going well for you there.

Best to you, & greetings from Carole—
Gary

January 25, 1996
Subject: New year greeting

Dear Gary,

I've come to the office from summer vacation to leave three boxes of books that we've cleared out from home: part of a big project of passing on / getting rid of excess STUFF. Last year I set up a Free Anarchist Bookstall outside my office, and these will go there. I (and now other people too) put books, magazines, etc. there, and students take them. A notice reminds them not to be greedy, and to bring back anything they don't want to keep. The idea is that these kids never read anything—in most cases they've never read a book that was not a prescribed setwork—so it's good to get things out to them.

I want to tell you about what has happened to one of my students: Shelley Barry, in my honours class on environmental literacy, a beautiful Asian / Spanish-looking girl, about twenty-two years old. A week ago she was shot. She was travelling with her partner, Janine, to campus in a minibus taxi. Someone (presumably from a rival taxi group) opened fire, and killed the driver. Then, with the taxi crashing towards a tree, he started shooting the passengers. She was shot twice. One bullet went through her shoulder and lodged into her spine. The other travelled through her chest, her lungs, and into Janine who was sitting next to her. It passed through her lungs and stopped millimetres from her heart. They are both alive, but Shelley is on a respirator in intensive care, and they say she won't walk again. She's been near death in the last few days, but it looks as if she will make it now. When I visited her yesterday, she said (mouthed silently, me lip-reading), "I feel good. There's so much love." Janine has been discharged, with a bullet lodged next to her heart. They say it's too dangerous to try and remove it. I'm telling you this because it's been such a terrible, absorbing thing to happen. Also, it gives you a sense of the context in which we're working. Shelley liked your poetry, and wrote a good essay on it last year. She's also done Tai Chi, taught English in Japan, where she'd hoped to return next year, and was very interested in Buddhism. She's an unusual person, her interests very different from that of 99.9 percent of the students we see. I've felt an obvious sort of connection with her, and am finding what has happened difficult to accept. The so-called Taxi-Wars are about access to routes. Most people travel on taxis these days, because it's the cheapest, most available form of transport, even if they drive dangerously and overload the minibus. The interests that own them are really gangsters, and this shooting is one example of the way they're beginning to operate: protect your route at any cost. At the moment, it's a strange comfort to me to recognise that I CAN'T understand why it happened to Shelley. We're adept at explaining, psychologising away all kinds of suffering, but this resists that sort of approach. I don't understand. If this here now is the Pure Buddha Land, what sense do we make of this pain? It's easy to feel equanimity about someone else's pain, but how presumptuous that can be. I can't understand. Trying to understand doesn't seem appropriate. What we have here now is a young girl in a hospital bed who's asking me for books and tapes. That's what I can respond to. This all has something to do with the Four Noble Truths, no doubt, but I can't quite work it out.

Hope you're all well, and that winter work is going well. I saw in *Tricycle* that you've done a new book. Is this so?

All good wishes to you all.

Love,

Julia

March 26, 1996

Dear Julia,

The account of what happened to Shelley. How very painful and sad, and what a waste. How is she doing now? If she is coming along, and it would not be a burden, I'd send her a note, a letter, a poem—

I'm so slow in answering this because I hadn't yet learned how to store mail in the "mailbox" folders that come with this software, and your letter got misplaced in the wrong mailbox file. I finally found my way into it, like some dungeons and dragons game. I appreciated your open and searching letter, and was much touched by it.

I sent you my recent *A Place in Space* and another book (not by me). I think they went sea-mail, but they should be there by now . . . & I have been showing your "Interbeing and the 'I' Habit" essay to colleagues here. There is a whole cluster of curricula in there. [. . .]

I am teaching on "the long poem" this spring, in fact teaching, to some degree, my own long poem. See below—

You are doing really good, and needed, work.

Love, Gary

March 28, 1996

Subject: Equinox, Autumn, Spring

Dear Gary,

How nice to find your message on my email screen yesterday, and a fat package of books on my desk today. Thank you. These are two books that I've been wanting to read, and they're not available here, so I very much appreciate your sending them. What a good surprise.

You asked about Shelley. She's better than she was in January, but they say she'll never walk again. The spinal cord is severed, or so they believe. There's a miniscule chance that it isn't, but they can't do the test to find out because there are pieces of metal in her body from the bullet which would interfere with the test. The paralysis is high too, so she can't move or feel anything below her breasts. After the initial high of morphine and survival, she became deeply depressed. She wouldn't look at people or speak or eat. When she started to talk she said to me, "Julia, this is a nightmare." She said, "I miss my cat. I miss my life. I really, really miss my life." I asked her what it felt like, and she said, "Like rocks, it's as though I'm weighed down by incredibly heavy rocks." I suggested she write about it, I suggested that she trust in the possibility of another state of mind, I found that I was trying to make things better, unable to stay with the reality of what she was suffering. Now it's a bit different. She has "good days" and "not so good days." She has a perspective on a range of states of mind rather than being sunk in one reality, and she's learning to use a wheelchair. She said to me last week, "I'm really curious to find out why this had to happen, what this is about." Being with her demands a completely no-bullshit presentness. Her dark eyes are open, her face is very pale, the hospital is old and dirty, patients and staff discriminate against her because she speaks English, is middle-class, doesn't eat meat. The pain is honest, the paralysis uncompromising. I said, "You're having to start from the beginning again." "Yes," she said, "I'm starting from the beginning all over again." I'm sure she would love to hear from you.

I do like the sound of the Long Poems course you're going to teach—wish I could attend. [. . .]

*May 15, 1996
Subject: Our spring, your fall*

Dear Julia,

An intense two months here. My mother just turned

*Responds to extracts from the previous email

ninety & then was diagnosed with a recurrence of breast cancer, which has now been removed & we'll see how long that holds. She has been up (a little) and down a lot. And then this is my teaching quarter & I'm driving back and forth between Davis and the ridge.

Hope you and Michael are well . . . my heart goes out to Shelley. And I will try to locate a useful contact at UC Berkeley on the chance she might want to go there. You are aware I'm sure that the UC system is in terrible financial shape (and that affirmative action's days seem to be numbered) so it's hard to say what the outlook might be. Will let you know. I'll send something to Shelley via you. I regret it has taken me so long to get back to you.

I'd be interested to hear the Blue Sky tape you have. It's true. Readings are uneven (what is the other one you have, Watershed?). I intend to listen to past readings as I prepare to go out and give new readings from the completed book this fall. I've learned a few things in the process of teaching this spring seminar on the long poem . . . a) Whitman is really amazing & was in some way a very realized person. b) Pound's *Cantos* is truly a failure. The loveliest lines in the *Cantos*, musically, are based on the seven-character poetic line. c) Williams's *Paterson* is also unsatisfying. A lot of flailing about & I don't much like the Harry Truman tone. d) And I still can't stand Stevens. A prissy metaphysical.

e) Eliot has more heart that I had remembered & a measured wisdom.

So I'm particularly impressed by Whitman's staying power. And am now curious to look again at the generation right after Pound and Eliot, Elizabeth Bishop's generation, and see who the strongest voices are. As for *Mountains and Rivers*, it is too weird to try to place at this point in literary history. But I feel strongly now that it's not a continuation of the Pound / Williams project, an idea I might have uncritically given assent to a few months ago.

[JM] I'm interested in the Whitman / William Carlos Williams / Stevens / Snyder constellation. I've been thinking peripherally about Williams ("no ideas but in things," "not ideas about the thing but the thing itself") and Stevens ("the evading metaphor," supreme fictions) in relation to the postmodern assertions about textuality, "nothing outside the text," etc. I mean, later in the year, to write something about this with regard to the representation of place / ecosystem, situatedness, home / homelessness in your work, and I'd planned to focus on *M&R*, continuing in some way on what I started on "The Blue Sky" in an essay a while ago.

[GS] I hope you will do this. And in spite of what I say about some of them. I'm going to send you a copy of an interesting diss. by Sharon Jaeger, John Hopkins, on the rhetorical strategies of *Practice of the Wild*.

[JM] About your visit (one day, next year I hope) to South Africa. I'm beginning to give up on the USIS. Another possible source of funding is the South African Centre for Science Development which gives grants for visits by "foreign research fellows." I think this is certainly a way to go. If you agree, I'd need a CV ("Details should be supplied in connection with exceptional achievements, publications and work during the last five years"), and we'd need to describe what you'll be doing here in terms of a collaborative "research programme," involving, for example, a "research problem." It wouldn't be difficult to describe your ongoing work in terms that show its relevance to research and teaching that is being done here, both at tertiary level and in work with communities. What do you think?

[GS] I'll work on the above. Could fulfill their requirements, I think. My research problem would have to do with representations of large wild animals in silhouette. First I saw them on the morning and evening horizon in Botswana, & felt genetic tugs, then I saw their forms at the Matopos rock art in Zimbabwe, & in June / July Carole and I are going with Clayton Eshleman and some clients to look at cave paintings in the Dordogne. There is a poem or an essay in all of this, all beings circulating & circumambulating the universe, & another visit to Africa would help—just to see a little more rock art, if nothing else. Back to you soon.

I do hope you get your half-year teaching schedule. As one who has done it now for ten years, it's ideal.

About ASLE, and next year . . . when would you be coming? I'm going to teach a poetics course next spring which I may title "Poetics of Practice." And I intend to design and present some very strong, long, readings of *Mountains and Rivers* & would hope you could see one. Actually, what would it take, I wonder, to do a visiting faculty member at some point and get to Davis for a year or a quarter. I should check around on this campus to find out. If you were involving me, say, in some of your research, it would be hopefully more justified. [. . .]

Interesting times here. It now feels as though the new right-wing Republican domination of Congress may be short-lived. The public does not want the environment to be totally trashed. But, of course, everything stays in the hands of the centrist pragmatist multinationals behind all scenes, for whom environmental degradation is also a problem. *Mountains and Rivers* is an offering of a totally different way to see the planet. With some of the steps as to how to get there written into it. But who wants to listen except the choir?

Carole and I and our families cannot complain. Our own lives are blessed, in terms of the pain of the world. Send me your project description . . . be well . . . love, Gary.

Julia / Michael,

Your package just arrived. Thank you for everything, the books, poems, clippings on tracking, the photos of your and your mother's artwork, the rock art. What a great-looking landscape. And I'd never seen a picture of Michael before. Michael, thank you for the Blue Buddha, the shell, the flakes. I look forward to absorbing it all.

I'll give you a report on the trip to France and what I learned about rock art there in the near future. I haven't quite gotten even a brief account together yet. Shortly after we got back from France, Carole checked in with her doctor & found a recurrence of a previous condition that requires surgery (going in next week) and a half-year of chemotherapy. It's a nonmalignant, slow-growing cell type, so this is not immediately life-threatening, but she has a mass in her abdomen that must be removed & then all the leftover cells killed so it won't grow back again. I cut my Japan trip down so that I only stayed over two nights, giving a lecture, visiting with Nanao, and coming right back. I have a fieldwork class from Davis that will be in residence here in the mountains in September, & that takes some preparation. So it's a dicey time right now. And this is fire season: smoky air everywhere from some big fires to the west cleaning up the Coast Range chaparral.

Hard to say just how far I might take a study of rock art, mainly to see it as part of a poem / essay I might do on the procession of animals as witnessed by humans in the moment, or over the last four decamillennia. And the procession of yaks and people that circumambulate the Himalaya, Pradakshina, circumambulation, a great practice. I don't want to go to a lot of trouble getting grants for this sort of thing. I'll play it loose for the nonce.

How was H. H.'s [His Holiness the Dalai Lama's] visit? What an honor for you to chair the meeting. He is surely the most respect-worthy, maybe the only, of internationally known world figures. It must have been wonderful for everyone. Please do tell me a little about it. And I will tell you how things go here. . . . Yr friend, Gary.

November 12, 1996

Dear Julia,

I've been meaning to answer you for several weeks. It's still a pretty hectic time for us as I both travel and teach, and try to help out Carole with chores around the place. We've got firewood in at least, and have drained most of the outside water lines for winter—burned the brush piles—that sort of thing. I just came back from three days in New York City, spent a little time with old Allen G. [Ginsberg], who has moved into a roomy new place with all his bookshelves up, much more light than he had before. He's very happy with that.

I was moved and touched by your account of hosting the Dalai Lama. I get the sense of a very dedicated—possibly beleaguered—progressive Buddhist circle of friends there. I also enjoyed your and Michael's account of the countryside, and the mountains and canyons. [. . .]

I will be going to the ASLE meeting, of course, just before that to at least part of the Squaw Valley Art of the Wild week, and just before that a few days in Tokyo for their big annual music and poetry festival. I'm not quite sure what you're thinking of, when you speak of coming to Davis and observing / teaching? I wish we had better things to show for our work here, the Nature and Culture courses—with the exception of the senior-level course, which I'm helping teach right now—are pretty elementary. That is, we have to ground students in some very basic methodology of science and criticism before we can get into the active stuff. For example, the dialogue between postmodern critics and naive environmentalists is something the instructors in the courses can barely get the students up to, because they first have to learn the terms of the discourse, and that's hard enough. The good thing is, we are not pushing students into trendy discussions of theory before they have mastered the terms of the discussion. So only a few are ready for ecofeminism, or Dharma connections with nature thought, or even ready to make much use of the critical theory / postmodern vocabulary. In fact there's a considerable resistance to it as obscurantist. Still, deep ecology does arouse a lot of curiosity, and bioregionalism and watershed work they take to like a sandhill crane takes to a recently harvested rice field. So the advanced class does have students who are out there working on plenty of good, very concrete questions—different projects and papers from our residence in the mountains in September. Nothing quite like that will be happening in May or June, though. Still, Davis is a huge university, and our broad committee of Nature and Culture faculty members ranges over plenty of territory, and someone who wanted to be around for while and talk to these different folks, touch into some of their different fields, could have a very exciting time.

Well, let me know what you're thinking, and I'll help in any way I can. Katsu Yamazato says he's going to try to make it over from Japan for the ASLE meeting too. My best to you and Michael—Carole sends hearty friendly greetings—& hello too to Michael, Gary.

Subject: Greetings from Julia (and a question)

Dear Gary,

Greetings from the midwintery world: day after day of welcome rain, garden growing greenly, fire in the hearth, children riding bicycles inside the house. I think of you so often, and I just haven't written. My computer seems permanently to have lost its wits, and my email address has evaporated. Meant to phone on your birthday to say hello, but then the day slipped by and the moment was gone. I hope you're well, and that Carole is as well as she can be.

The big change in our lives recently was to move out of Mowbray where we'd been in the same house for eighteen years, and come to a place called Muizenberg. Have I mentioned this before? It's a bit out of the city, but still accessible for a longish commute to work for me. The house is part of a narrow old built corridor surrounded by wilderness: sea, wetland, and mountain. Muizenberg is a small seaside town, good swimming beaches, the mountain five minutes' walk from our front steps, big wetland close by, much clearer air, big garden by local standards, old house, space for sandpit,

*Five years later: . . . computers crashed and stolen, no proper backup, many letters lost.

swing, wendy house, vegetable garden, trees to climb, and many exploring places. [. . .]

The pressure at work is on for us to Publish and Do Research. Our universities have tyrannical and silly ways of rewarding and punishing us with regard to publications, and they don't recognise "creative" writing in their sums. Michael says I'm crazy not to try and get the doctorate published in some form, and perhaps he's right. As soon as I've finished writing something, I seem to lose interest in trying to get it published. It's the writing that's the interesting part. And at the moment I haven't been doing any of that. I think that writing my thesis while taking care of such small babes, and teaching at the same time . . . sort of emptied out the part of my brain that does that sort of thing. So I went rather blank for a while, then we moved house, and now I don't have any clear idea of what academic writing to do next, or even how to keep going with what I've been doing all along. My mind is tired, and full of children, and the growing of vegetables. It's a funny question, perhaps (and it's only just occurred to me to ask you), but can you think of a question / idea "with heart" that you imagine I should / could follow up? Or can you suggest a way of waking up the researcher / writer in the mind? How to get going with a chicken-coop (remember somewhere you said that sort of writing is like building one)? I'd rather write essays than straight articles. Anyway, you understand the work I've done so far better than most people and you've always been a teacher for me. So here's the student asking for some pointers. I suppose there's a bit of spiritual stuckness somewhere in there too: the "completed" written task is empty yet seems pretentious, "I" don't have much to say, etc. Maybe I shouldn't get my "practice" life tangled up with the academic one—but what else is really interesting? Not two?

Hmmm. This email has taken an unexpected turn.

I was reading the other night to Michael your narrative about Kitkitdizze in *The Gary Snyder Reader*. We loved the 300-year-plan for tree planting, etc., and I remembered, vaguely, something I once read about a college at Oxford. New College, perhaps? A few years ago it was found that the vast, ancient oak beams from which it was constructed needed replacing. What to do? The stuff doesn't just grow on trees anymore. . . . Then someone found a document locating a forest of oaks that had been planted on College lands, hundreds of years before. The people who built the place knew that the beams would need replacing around now, and had planted the trees at the time to provide for just this.

The babes continue to delight and exhaust and amaze us. Boy / girl stereotypes abound. Apparently testosterone levels double in the boy's bloodstream around the fourth birthday (now). This evening I'd been helping Sky build a complicated garage out of Lego. When I was out of the room, Sophie stomped on the garage and went upstairs. I helped him rebuild it, and then (after, it turned out, a reading of *Peter Rabbit* this morning by Granny) she came downstairs with arms full of toy rabbits that she'd managed to find around the house. Mommy, daddy, and twin rabbits all cuddly and nice. She and Michael played a rabbit game with them. Next thing, Sky stomped on garage number two, and turned a part of it into a gun. "Whoosh! I shoot rabbits!" Sophie runs, panicking, to me in the kitchen. "Whoosh! I've got a special gun!" (Never really worked out what a gun was before, but it seems that he got some ideas from Beatrix Potter.) Sophie, "What does it shoot?" Sky, "Rabbits! Whoosh" (lunge, shriek, etc.). Towards the end of it all, he said, "Now I'm a very kind man who does this to guns" (break, stamp, stomp on Lego).

Gary—this is long enough. My love to you and Carole.

Xxoxo J

September 23, 2001

Subject: Spring / autumn equinox

Dear Gary,

How are you doing? We've just returned from a week walking in the abundant joy of spring flowers up the West Coast, and all the news is of America and global crisis. Our hearts feel for the victims of the atrocity, but it's alarming to think that the man who wouldn't agree to pollution controls ("because the American way of life is not up for negotiation") is at the helm.

Please note my new email address.

Thinking of you and Carole and your children.

With much love,

Julia

December 14, 2001

Dear Julia and Michael,

I'm looking at this postcard from September that has a solid field of flowers reaching out almost as far as one can see. That must be what John Muir was describing in his essay "The Bee Fields of California" when he spoke of how the Great Central Valley—before it was plowed, drained, and converted into agribusiness—was a solid field of flowers for tens of miles in every direction, farther than you could see. Your postcard made it real for us.

We are steady on course, with Carole's reduced energy and me trying to handle the mounting karmic pressures of being rather too well known, and still get the real work done. Ah, the real work. I have a few worthy little projects still to

---

*Snyder did respond about 9/11, but the email has been lost.

cover—and will be leaving teaching at the university after this spring to, as I tell people, "get back to work." Or play—I told Daniel Ellsberg (of *The Pentagon Papers*) over ten years ago that the sixties were for one to finish their work in, and one's seventies were to play. I haven't really gotten around to playing much yet in my seventies, but then my work is my play. I hope you and the kids are well. Hear you are having a good summer solstice to match our winter solstice. I'm still thinking of the research, meditation, and poetry I want to do on the matter of ancient cave art and rock art—when I get to it. I certainly will let you know if and when it looks like I could come for a visit to South Africa. I'd love to. But I can't do as much as I would have, because Carole can't travel, and I don't want to leave her for too long.

Blessings,

Gary

April 3, 2002
Subject: From Julia

Dear Gary,

[...] It's autumn now, the children singing "Summer Goodbye . . ." a song they learnt at their Waldorf kindergarten. Although rather peopled with gnomes and water nixies, the worldview they're absorbing there seems the most congenial educational one around at present. I'm working towards writing an essay about little boys for a book coming out in the US called *Men and Nature*. Specifically, the question that I'm thinking about is to do with how we can help our little boys grow up to be men who are compassionate, imaginative, wise, and brave. How, practically, to cultivate both insight into interdependence and the sympathetic imagination—or versions of wisdom and compassion. Again and again, it seem to me that our middle-class boys (especially in SA?) inherit an ideology which, through the value placed on aggressive and competitive self-assertion, prepares them to be part of the problem of ecosocial degradation rather than agents of healing and transformation. A lot of current writing on boy-raising seems to be using an essentialist brain science approach to focus on TESTOSTERONE as the innate ingredient that almost inevitably promotes competitive and aggressive self-assertion. Although . . . actually parenting a boy does make you wonder, especially when he has a twin sister around for comparison. Years ago when we did that interview, I remember glibly asserting that boy-girl differences were all due to socialisation. You said something like no, prior to socialisation. Not that all boys are wired to love machines, but that the patterning of specific identity is something each person brings into the world from birth.

Living in South Africa at the moment is perplexing. Where we are, you can hear the sea and walk up on to the mountain with the children. Many birds visit the garden, and we grow our own vegetables. Neighbours are friendly. There's a wonderful bakery and café nearby and many beaches. At the same time, this country has the highest rate of HIV infection in the world—among the communities where my students come from, one in four people is now infected—yet the government appears to be in a state of aggressive denial. There's also a lot of violent crime and poverty, at many levels, and not too much respect for democracy. We've stopped getting a daily newspaper and don't have television, so don't feel as battered by the repetitious negativity that these media tend to promote. Yet friends, once again, are talking of emigrating and it's unsettling. Otherwise, we're well.

Love to you and Carole,

Julia

*September 2002

Thinking of you, & hoping you're well.

A family of porcupines run across our path in the night, quills raised in a spikey fan of alarm. Sophie says I should also tell you about the hare and the owl, the buck, the dassie (hyrax), & the mouse. We come here every year, & it's always familiar & always new—so wonderful. The twins, now five,

*Postcard: Spring flowers in Namaqualand

play hide & seek on the rocks & point out what they're see-
ing. As always, your writing about wildness returns to mind.

XO with much love, Julia

November 8, 2002
Subject: Existential Q

Hi Julia,

The first winter storm has come in off the Pacific and hit
the West Coast with strong winds and an inch or so of rain.
The annual summer dry spell is over. We've been almost
a month on the Mendocino coast in a friend's house, just
Carole and me, I'm trying to catch up on editing & articles.
And doing some poems. It's the way to get some work done,
no doubt. Carole's health stays the same, always on the edge,
always uncomfortable, but stable for the time.

I've been thinking about your query below. I know the
problem well. I hope you can relax with your life and the
family needs, and trust your long-range life pattern to
bring you back to your work when you're ready. Meantime,
jot down a few haiku in the gaps. At least, I found, during
several-year-long spells in Japan when I wasn't writing, if I
tried doing the other things at hand and giving them good
energy, it worked out in the long run.

You should try and get your doctorate published, but it
would take a round of editing that would point it to a chosen
audience. And it is not really urgent.

[JM]* It's a funny question, perhaps (and it's only just occurred to me to ask you), but can you think of a question / idea "with heart" that you imagine I should / could follow up? Or can you suggest a way of waking up the researcher / writer in the mind? How to get going with a chicken-coop (remember somewhere you said that sort of writing is like building one)?

[GS] I'd say more to the point is who you are and what your life is in the present moment which is close to practice, but without big expectations. I've turned to little anecdotal haibun (i.e., prose + poem) exercises lately, which have as their idea mainly just "heart." The heartfelt moments of the recent past that don't get into other prose or poetry. (I've also done a few articulate forestry issue articles, local to the West Coast.) But for most of the seven years since *Mountains and Rivers* came out I've done very little writing or research and have sort of fielded questions from people, looked after Carole and also my very ancient mother, taken care of the place, and taught at Davis. And as of last summer, I'm done with that, too.

Child raising is huge work. Don't blame yourself if you can't do everything. Carole would tell you that too; she tried to be a supermom in the late seventies with a job running the clinic for migrant families, righteous community politics, big family of relatives, lots of footloose friends, running

*Portions of July 11, 2001 email are repeated here (labeled JM) preceding responses (labeled GS).

a commercial orchard, and two daughters. Her marriage fell apart, and she stepped back. She now feels she was trying for an impossible and unnecessary model. Pick and choose your targets.

[JM] The completed written task is empty yet seems pretentious, "I" don't have much to say, etc. Maybe I shouldn't get my "practice" life tangled up with the academic one—but what else is really interesting? Not two?

[GS] Here's where you shouldn't sell yourself short. Put a finished work aside for some months, and then look at it afresh. It won't be pretentious, or if it seems to be, put it aside for another period of time. If it's ready, you'll see what rewrites it needs, and you'll feel proud of your work. If it still looks unsatisfactory after, say, eighteen months, put it in another drawer and forget about it. Move on. At least that's what I and a few others I know do—

Hope this is some help to you.

Little haibun below,

Fondly, Gary

May 8, 2003

Subject: Happy Birthday

Dear Gary,

Happy birthday, my friend. Every day is a good day, but I'm glad this day brought you into the world, along with all the delightful gifts of wisdom and fun and generosity that came with you.

I thought about you this morning as I was walking for about two hours in the early light along the coast near here: a seal playing in the water, oyster catchers on the rocks, an old Khoi [Khoisan] fish trap made of rocks, line fishermen smiling good morning, and the waves flowing forever. It's so wonderful to live here. Looked for a postcard to send, but none of the tourist stuff could picture it.

Michael's polishing a pendant of Jupiter in his workshop under the house, while Sky watches. Sophie is tucking a family of small bears to bed in the doll's house.

We're leaving, I hope, at the end of the month for our expedition to the Northern Cape. We'll send you something.

Thanks for the piece about Coyote Man and the President. Beautiful. Are you interested in doing another interview some time? Maybe next year?

My love to you and Carole.

Julia

June 10, 2003
Subject: Old stone heart

Dear Gary,

What can I tell you about our expedition. . . . We have visited some very powerful places whose deep, old silence resists whatever stories we'd like to tell about them. Still, one likes to speak. I'm starting a longish prose piece about the journey which I'll send some time, but here are a few notes. The area is the Northern Cape: in the geographical heart of the country, around the city of Kimberley, and near Kuruman, 200 kilometres away. Dry, thorny, semi-deserty land. Some places:

- Canteen Kopje—site of the first alluvial diamond digging, which turned up one of the richest known hand axe locations—an estimated 100 million artefacts. They're old, some tumbled by ancient rivers, and going back to about 1.2 million years ago. The biggest hand axes (ever yet) were found here: massive things we held in the museum. The longest (38.5cm) and the heaviest (7.7kg). Archaeologists found fragments of specularite here (a sort of starry glitter) which comes from 200 kilometres away, right down in the 250,000 layer. It was precious stuff, put in the hair, traded, and invariably used in Late Stone Age burials, on the hair. Head full of stardust. Someone has reckoned they were using it 400,000 years ago.
- Wildebeestkuil—Beautiful engravings of buck and elephants and people and patterns on the rocks at the top of a koppie. A San man (whose people come from Angola,

but there is some cultural continuity) interprets them for us, and talks about their relation to the trance: gathering power from the animals so as to be able to "see into your body, so that I can draw the arrows of sickness out."

- Nooitgedacht glacial pavement—Big expanse of rock with more engraved patterns, and the trace of a glacier.

- Driekopseiland—A wonderful, very wide, grey expanse of rock in a river, which is covered with about 3,500 engravings, almost all "geometric" patterns of flow and radiating lines rather than being representational. The oldest are about 2,500 years old, the most recent maybe 200 or slightly less. We spent the time there with archaeologist David Morris, who's studied them. He thinks the rock is the watersnake, and believes the engravings to have something to do with women's initiation: after first menstruation, a young woman might go to the river to wash, and then make her mark on the rock.

- Wonderwerk Cave—A vast, great, dark tunnel into a hillside, where archaeologists led by Peter Beaumont have done a lot of excavation. In fact they've pretty much ripped up the whole cave except the final cavern, which is yet undiscovered (leading me to think quite a bit about what happens when a place becomes a site . . .). It's all gridded up with lines of string. But the information they've discovered is awesome too. Peter showed us the ash low down from the fires 1 million years ago. Charred bones were found in the fireplaces. There's also a layer of bedding from 400,000 BP (they can detect the grass from silica traces), and even actual grasses preserved from 200,000 BP (BP = Before the Present, i.e., 1950 when carbon dating began). They also found a layer of quartz crystals as well as other semiprecious stones collected some distance away. Peter, who believes that the Northern Cape is "where it all began," says that the cave is the only place in the world which we know of that was inhabited from 1.2 million years ago to 100 years ago (when a local farmer lived there with his family).

- The Kuruman Eye—An oasis in the desert, a beautiful clear-water spring which gives the town of Kuruman free water, and is the home of certain fish (nobody quite knows how they got there). It must have been a treasured place for the ancestors.

- Kathu Townlands—The site which sparked our curiosity. Billions of very ancient lithic artefacts (nobody knows how many as the area is vast, but Peter has consistently uncovered 9,000 per cubic metre). The part you can see is an area that was ground up for road gravel—the rest is grass covered. We wandered, picked them up, put them down [. . .] the place is unspeakable. No stories, really, just all those tools.

- Blinkklipkop—An ancient specularite mine, where people have been collecting starry rock and red ochre since the Middle Stone Age. Both of these "nonfunctional"—for ritual or cosmetic purposes. In recent history, the specularite was guarded by shamans, and could be traded for cattle.

These are the official sites we visited. Otherwise, we found worked stones on the railway line outside Kimberley, on roadsides everywhere and all over the hill on a game farm near Kuruman. Michael also found a piece of engraved rock in the heap of stones and Early Stone Age artefacts where a water pipe had been dug at the game farm. Took it back to the museum. "Most extraordinary," David said. He'll follow it up. Someone called the museum with the find of a fossil dinosaur skull, and we went with Peter to see it. Meanwhile, David was excavating some 100-year-old skeletons just discovered in a mass burial in Kimberley, probably from a mining disaster. There was also a lake with about 25,000 flamingoes chattering to each other in it.

There are many other sites in the area that we didn't visit. I'd like to go again. And I'd really like you to come too. I understand that you're not doing much travelling, but I know you'd be happy to see these places of the ancestors.

Michael dreams of hand axes every night, and I dreamt my grandfather had stone stools in his study. On my desk is a small and mottled stone, an old stone heart, a tool.

Much love to you and Carole.

Julia

February 6, 2004
Subject: a thought

Dear Gary,

Late summer days here, swimming and ripe fruit.

I've been thinking again about the possibility of an interview. Thank you again for agreeing to talk some time. My dilemma is that I'd really like to meet with you but am still very much involved in the dailyness of small children. At six, they've just started school [. . .]. So . . . what to do? The trip to the US seems like such a long way, and I suddenly had the odd thought that you might be going to be somewhere closer to here, Europe perhaps, this year, and I could meet you there. Is this at all likely? What do you think?

My love to you and Carole.

Julia

April 8, 2005
Subject: tonglen

Dearest Gary and Carole,

A teaching from our friend Fiona Anderson that I would like to share with you—much love from Julia.

Fiona is Sky's godmother, Michael is her daughter Anna's godfather, and we've done a lot of small-child parenting things together. She is a tiny, fine-boned person with long blond hair who is not Alice in Wonderland whom she much resembles, but a GP and homeopath and a rather fearless person who climbs a lot of mountains, likes sleeping out under the stars, and has been doing some Buddhist practice. She is married to Staz, an ex-Bolshoi ballet dancer. Yesterday she arrived here and told us this story.

For the Easter holiday the three of them took her parents' old Land Cruiser up to the northernmost part of the country: wild foresty parts near the Mozambique border. They were late getting to the camp, travelling at night on a pot-holed, narrow dirt road, when they were stopped by three guys with guns who pulled them out of the car and made them lie on the road. Hijack. Anna, seven years old like our twins, was still in the vehicle. When Fiona said she wanted her child with her, they said, "No, we'll kill you." "OK, kill me," she said, "but I must have my child." Anna heard this, darted out past the men, and went to Fiona: "Now they won't kill you, Mommy."

Fiona then told Anna, guns against their heads, "OK, now we're not going to fight anymore. I only fought because I wanted you. We're not in charge of this, and they're not in charge of it either. God is in charge. If God wants us back, and this is our time to die, then that is how it is and it is fine. And I can promise you that dying is just like a change of tune. And if God only takes Daddy and me, and you are left, you must wrap yourself in the blanket of God's love. Somebody will find you, and you will be looked after."

One guy took the car and all their stuff, and they were driven around for about an hour, lying on their faces in the back of the truck, guns everywhere. Fiona says she's never been so frightened. She speaks fluent Zulu and spoke to the men in their language. Otherwise, she knew that the only thing she could do was *tonglen*, the Tibetan practice: breathing in the blackness of the other person's pain and cruelty, and breathing out into him the pure white light of compassion. Driving, face down, *tonglen* all the way. Couldn't find Chenrezig so she put Jesus in her heart, shining out white light. The truck stopped, and one guy said to Fiona "OK, now I'm going to rape you and then I'm going to kill you." She told Anna not to watch, told Staz that she would be OK. Carried on doing *tonglen*. He pulled off her clothes, tried to do it, but nothing happened. Couldn't get it up. Finally, one of the others said, "You're wasting our time," and they were all back in the truck again.

One man drove the Land Cruiser away, over the border, while the younger man guarded the family. They got talking to him, Anna asking him why he does this sort of work, why doesn't he do the same work as his father used to do. They started talking about their fathers. Fiona did *tonglen* all night, while the others fell asleep, even the young man guarding them, his gun at his feet.

Hours later, the man who wanted to rape her took Fiona to the front of the truck and said, "Now I'm really going to do it, and then I'll kill you." Driving with one hand on the steering wheel, he started fiddling with her, and she continued with the *tonglen*. Told Anna to go to sleep. Then he stopped the car, and told the younger man to kill Staz. He took him out into the bush, and Fiona held her hands over Anne's ears so she wouldn't hear the shot. Nothing happened. Then she heard them coming back, talking. The driver said, "Now this is it, and I can tell you, I've got no fucking mercy." She did two big last *tonglen* breaths. And he fell asleep.

He slept for about an hour, Fiona doing *tonglen* all the time. She said that when he woke up, he looked like a human being again and she knew he wouldn't hurt her. The men left the three of them, carrying a little juice and water, in the middle of a forest in the middle of the night, nine hours after it all began. "Thank you, Mummy," the man said to Fiona.

The moon was down, but the sky was full of stars and they used the Southern Cross to find direction. An owl flew past and Anna said it dropped two falling stars, like owl poo. The forest was full of fireflies.

Much love to you and Carole.

Julia

May 14, 2005
Subject: Re: poems

Dear Julia,

Off to Korea shortly—I'll respond to these thoughts right now . . . and wishing you and Mike and the twins most well at the beginning of your winter.

Best to you all, Gary

[JM] Dear Gareth,

It was good to hear from you. I'd had one of those wakeful nights, mind spinning about, particularly in relation to the book I'm writing about the archaeological sites in the Northern Cape that we've been visiting. So I decided that I needed to shift gears by writing to you, finding out which

*Responds to an email

poems you wanted to read, and putting my attention into the ASLE trip. Then your email arrived first thing. So I spent the morning reading *Danger on Peaks* again, amid driving to rescue and be with my eighty-six-year-old mother who had fallen on her face, lots of bruising but otherwise OK. Is your mother still alive?

[GS] I hope your mother is OK, meaning, really, no broken bones. My mother, Lois Wilkie Snyder, died last August in her sleep, at age ninety-eight. I'm still reorganizing her house, which is in wretched shape from termites anyway.

[JM] Thank you for asking which poems I'd like you to read. I expected to respond to your choices, but since you ask, here are the ones (probably too many?) that I would choose: I think the framing sections, I and VI, clearly need to be there, although I'd make a choice from I: definitely "The Climb" and "Atomic Dawn," and then, say, "Some Fate," "1980: Letting Go," "Pearly Everlasting." I assume you'll want to read the whole of the wonderful "After Bamiyan."

[GS] I might not read quite all of those from Part I because I'm doing that whole set in a big way on May 18th in Portland at the twenty-fifth-anniversary reading for Mount St. Helens' eruption. But you'll be tuned for whatever ones I choose, clearly.

[JM] From section II, any of the delightful small poems ("How," "Cool Clay," etc.) would work well, I think, although probably again I might ask for the framing "Yet Older Matters" and "Sand Ridge."

[GS] good plan

[JM] From III there are several: "Summer of '97," "Really the Real," "Waiting for a Ride," and possibly "Winter Almond."

[GS] sure

[JM] IV: "For Philip Zenshin Whalen." V: "Night Herons," "The Acropolis Back When," "One Thousand Cranes."

[GS] Depending on how the time is looking I might add one or two more in, but I'll be watching to save time for "After Bamiyan." Three that I'll definitely read are the "coyote old man consults with his turds" sequence (a widespread western North American coyote tale motif), which are the poems on pp. 21, 59, 75. I'll have a brief comment on this motif at some point (but never pointing it out too obviously).

[JM] How does this sound? Too many, I suppose. Do let me know, and then I'll get on with putting something together.

[GS] Maybe a bit much, but let's be prepared. They're giving me forty-five minutes, and the rest of the ninety-minute slot divided between you and audience questions to us both.

[JM] My own comments will be framing this sequence of poems in terms of where do we go now with "literature of the environment." Even if they do expect me to speak "off the cuff," I'd rather come with a prepared response, and then be able to shift things as needed. The question I want to look at has to do with reading the collection in relation to the teenage Snyder's vow to "fight against this cruel destructive power and those who would seek to use it"—what sort of fight / resistance / intervention / affirmation is possible from the standpoint you have taken (nondualism, ecological sanity, long-term inhabitation, etc.), and how the poetry seems to work to evoke this by transforming the terms of oppositional discourse, shifting point of view into another territory, etc. I'm interested in the phrase "crossing the postmodern divide"—can you say more about it?

[GS] Good questions, Julia . . . people ask me about that vow & what happened, & I tell them it evolved into learning what having a "vow" means and entails, and discovering the "Bodhisattva's Four Vows," among others. (There's Blake's vow, for example.) I do hope the poetry evokes this, as you suggest, with the shifting discourse.

[JM] Michael said you might like to see some of the other work I'm doing at the moment—the reflective travel narrative about the Northern Cape—so I'm attaching one chapter. It refers at some point I think to the Bleek-Lloyd archive, which is an extraordinary collection of 12,000 pages of /Xam (San—Bushman) narratives translated into English in the 1870s, more or less the last recorded voices of that culture.

[GS] Thanks! I'll get to reading it when I get back from Korea.

[JM] With regard to our interview, would you like to see the further thoughts I've been having, or shall we just leave it until the time? I've had a look at the conference programme, but it looks utterly crammed and rather overwhelming—I'll be glad to miss some of the sessions, though the field trips sound as though they could be good. Should we make a time in advance, or see how it works when you arrive?

[GS] I'm in Eugene from the eve of the 23rd until early the 25th, as it stands now. Two nights at The Excelsior. I haven't yet seen the entire schedule. Maybe we could do the interview around 5:30pm and have dinner together after, you figure an hour is enough? Excelsior is 754 E. 13th, near campus, 342-6963. I'll get there by 4pm. So call me. There's a restaurant at the inn, among other things. Or we could find time the next morning.

Carole's not too well but gets to the important things. She'll be in Corvallis with Kai's family while I'm in Eugene, and then I'll rejoin them.

. . . G. (Gwaereth, in Goidelic. "Spear-bearer" I once read.)

∗ To go back to the wild is to become sour, astringent, crabbed. Unfertilized, unpruned, tough, resilient, and every spring *shockingly* beautiful in bloom.

Gary Snyder

Kitkitdizze
north of the South Yuba River

> Daowu asked Shitou, What's the main point?
>   said,—Not to attain, not to know.
> Daowu asked, What goes beyond even that?
>   said,—The sky doesn't stop the clouds from flying.

Early June 2005

Hi Gary—
Sorry, I thought I'd replied to this earlier. Thanks for your greetings to our family. My mother was, it turned out, really knocked emotionally by the fall I mentioned, although now seems to be mending. Winter has come with lots of rain, which is wonderful, although the dams are still only 30 percent full. I'm so looking forward to seeing you, and to our session at the conference. As regards the interview, how about I come to meet you at the Excelsior at 5pm on the 23rd and we do what we can of the interview after that—if there's more we want to talk about, and supper has intervened, we can make another time later. I'd prefer more than an hour, but let's see how it goes.

Love to all,
Julia

Early June 2005

Dear Julia,

I know I'll be seeing you soon, but I just finished reading the recently arrived *Western American Literature* with your essay on *Mountains and Rivers Without End*, and it is outstanding. Really up there. Xie xie ni.

Yrz, Gary

Late June 2005

Subject: how good to see you

Dear Gary,

How good it was to see you again. I felt that the small time we had together was enough to reconfirm the warm old friendship we share, and that in the more formal times of interview and public talk, the same connection remained. So thank you again for this.

The interview sounds good. I'll have it transcribed, do some editing, and then send it to you. Here attached is the longer version of what I prepared for the response after your reading. For the actual presentation, I shortened it, and then cut even further after Allison sent a note along the row to me to "be concise." So here it is.

Thank you for the package of things you gave me—recent essays, and the wonderful picture of the Bear Woman and her babies.

Best love to you, and especially to Carole.
Julia

p.s. I am thinking about how to respond to an email from a woman at the conference who objected to my comments about the United States and Babylon. She likes your poems, so I think I'll direct her towards the idea of Amerika in "Front Lines." It's an interesting thought for me, though. As a South African, I grew up in an environment dominated by state policies, which all people of conscience found abhorrent. If a writer / scholar / artist did visit the country during the dark days of apartheid (most stayed away—cultural boycott), there was an obvious moral obligation for him or her to take a clear stand against the dominant ideology. We expected and welcomed this, but perhaps United States citizens, brought up on vows of allegiance, don't. Even some critical people, at an environmental conference. Perhaps this is part of the problem.

July 2005

Dear Julia,

Such a pleasure, even such a short visit together, in Eugene. Just that thirty-six hours that I was there exhausted me. Such a crowd, and such energy. After I go over the schedule (of which I did not get a copy of my own until the

23rd), I'll see what I think was missing from the talks and presentations. I've already told you how much I liked your essay on *Mountains and Rivers*, and specifically, I much appreciate the usefulness and wisdom of invoking the "earth touching mudra"—and explaining what that moment meant, in the life of Shakyamuni, and in all of later Buddhism. Your interpretation of it is I think right on, and what a good way to say it. Also your observation that I do not play an adversarial role in head-on terms. It's necessary to look at all the angles and slip in from whatever side. In Japanese kendo, wooden sword fighting practice, they say that this is looking for the *suki*—the opening. The opening is where you get your chance. I would hope I have learned a few lessons and am able to apply coyote insights creatively in poetry—

The talk you did after my reading was simply the first thing I've heard about those poems that is thoughtful, is more than thoughtful, that gets it. I'm very grateful for that, too.

And by now, you must be back in Cape Town. Wendell Berry always said that if you go away for one week you'll be three weeks behind, all the stuff you didn't do before you left, what piled up while you were gone, and it keeps happening. And so I'm sure, with the twins too, you're pretty busy.

I'm hoping to get someone, maybe Eric Todd Smith, to

take on the organizing and editing job for a collection of essays on *Mountains and Rivers* that would include the four best I know—Tim Dean, you, Eric's booklet essay, and Kim Uchang's. I know I have read a few others, maybe not so notable, but I'll look for them and see what I think. And there may well be others out there—so if you can think of any candidates (ditto Eric and Tim), we'll see what we get. It might be time now to do that.

Back here, Carole has not been well and right now she's in the little local hospital getting some further tests and IV antibiotics and extra nutrition. We're hoping that this will shake her recent infections and put her back at least where she was able to do something creative every day.

Best wishes to Michael and the kids, hugs to you,

Gary

July 2005

Dear Gary,

Here's a working text of our interview in Eugene. [. . .]

I think it's an interesting piece, quite different really from the interview we did in 1988 that was published in *Tri-Quarterly*. Then it seemed more a case of powering through quite a range of issues. Now it's shorter (only twenty-five minutes) and seems lighter, easier, a gentle and direct reflection on some Really Big Questions. I haven't played around much with the order of the conversation because I like the organic flow from one idea to the next.

Let me know what you think.

August 2005

Dear Julia,

Carole is, remarkably, still hanging in with us. Report below. But I'm also writing you in regard to a point regarding your trip to Eugene in June. I know you were intending to get some university support for your round-trip transportation? Did that go through OK? Would it be of any help to you if I wrote you a personal letter describing our event on the 24th and thanking you specifically for your participation in my program and the quality of your statement?

As for the interview—what with caretaking Carole and all of her family, I haven't had a chance to really read it. I hope to in the next couple of weeks—

Hope all's well with you, Michael, and the kinder.

Love, Gary

Carole is still with us. Surprising to all, Carole's spartan home regimen of no more antibiotics and no more tube feeding has served her well. She has eaten only bites of morsels for over two weeks and is down to eighty pounds but for seven days now has stayed steady at that. She's on regular pain medication, but not so much that she's too spacey. So her life has smoothed out, and she's hanging in for a while longer, with pleasure in each day. The new baby quilt project is almost finished! Carole's not answering the phone or seeing people except by impulsive invitation but otherwise enjoying an almost normal daily life for a few more days or weeks. We've had many very sweet notes and messages of everyone's love and concern. The world is woven it seems of both gratitude and sorrow together. Most family members have had to go back to their lives in the Valley and in San Francisco, and I have learned how to administer various medications. Carole says, "I'm enjoying this world a lot, and maybe I'll write something about my grandfather." We'll see how daily life goes –

Love from us here, Gary

August 2005
Subject: Tara

Dearest Gary,

You and Carole are so much in our thoughts. Such tender days.

After receiving your email this morning about her, I spent

most of the day stitching a quilt for a new baby who was born a week ago. Our friends, first-time parents, sounded wobbly, happy, and vulnerable when I called.

So with all of you particularly in mind, these lines from a Hymn to Tara:

> I bow to you, of the colour of the harvest moon:
> Full is your face, made of a hundred moons.
> From you shines the light of a thousand stars.
> Radiant, flaming with glory, I bow before you.
> Wearing yellow and blue lotuses, with hands like
>   water-lilies;
> lotuses in your hands, always adorned with flowers.
> Generous; full of energy; patient in ascetic practice:
> full of the peace of meditation.
> Enduring all, with mind one-pointed; the essence of
>   perfect activity.
> To you, I bow, the crest jewel of the Tathagatas,
>   those who have gone beyond.

How very kind of you to wonder about my travel costs at this time. All is completely fine—my university paid. As for our interview, I just wanted to get it transcribed and send it off to you. Of course, there's absolutely no hurry for you to get around to looking at it.

My love to Carole and to you,
Julia

Hi Julia,

Carole is hanging in, almost off all medication, eating just enough to survive, and very clear and bright. I'm her sole caregiver now.

I tried to print out your paper, "The path that goes beyond," and it will not print out, whatever tricks I try. It shows signs of being in a software I don't know, and my printer, an Epson that prints out a variety of softwares, somehow doesn't recognize whatever yours is. I'm curious, what is it? And, could you send the paper again in something like Word or Appleworks or whatever?

Today we're picking some fresh tomatoes & skinny Japanese eggplant / brinjal / aubergines / na-tzu / nashi—so tasty grilled and with fresh ginger!

Gary

> "Mind itself is buddha"—difficult to practice,
> but easy to explain;
> "No mind, no buddha"—difficult to explain,
> but easy to practice.
>
> —Dogen

October 7, 2005
Subject: last bit of light editing

Dear Gary,

It was good to hear your news about Carole. I hope you all had a wonderful birthday.

Would you mind having another look at this attachment and letting me know what you think? I've put in your changes to the interview, given it a title (I think it's OK, but maybe you can suggest a better one?), and made some minor alterations to my comments / questions. Sometimes I was still responding to something which you had now edited out! Not sure what you want to do about dating it—see my note on light editing at the end. [. . .]

I've been having a challenging time with my eighty-seven-year-old mother. On Sunday she dislocated her hip, and in order to get it back in place she was put under anaesthetic. On waking up in the hospital she became incredibly and uncharacteristically confused and angry ("dementia," the doctors helpfully like to call it), thinking that we'd put other people in her apartment, taken away her things, etc. It's all to do with a sense of disorientation and understandable fears of losing control of her life. Since then sanity seems gradually to be returning, and she's back home with a temporary nurse-aide looking after her. Still, she's pretty muddled and weak, and the doctors are saying she can't live alone anymore (she's in a retirement place, but not in constant care). So . . . I'm sure this scenario and the distress it brings is fairly familiar to you. I don't have any brothers or sisters to help make decisions or take charge, so am feeling a bit jangled by it all. Still, it always helps to breathe and smile and have a good laugh. Looking out my window, the sky is very blue, and a pair of yellow butterflies are chasing one another in the wind.

Love to you and Carole.

Julia

October 8, 2005

Subject: Re: last bit of light editing

Dear Julia,

What did I edit out that you were responding to? I might have missed it.

Otherwise, it looks fine to me. [. . .] As for dating it, maybe it would be simple to just leave it with the original June date.

I can empathize with you and your mother. It gets very hard. Several people who were advisors to people taking care of elders told me, several times over, not to feel guilty, to keep my own sanity, and to remember my mother as she was when younger, not as she was in her last years. We have to make, sometimes, some hard decisions. All that was helpful—I wish you luck. Getting firewood for winter in with my son Gen lately—warmly, Gary

> Hit absolute rock bottom
> Are you there rock? No?
> No rock on bottom
> —Joanne Kyger

Gary Snyder
Kitkitdizze
north of the South Yuba River
near the headwaters of Blind Shady Creek
in the trees at the high end of a bunchgrass meadow.

Mid-October 2005
Subject: thank you

Dear Gary,

[. . .] Thank you for your empathy about the situation with my mother. It's been a difficult week. She dislocated her hip a second time after I last wrote and went into hospital. The doctor called me and said he wanted to operate, but I must understand that it could be fatal. He thought that she was wrenching the hip out with an involuntary jerk. Remembering how really traumatic a previous hip operation was for her, I said well, let's try and treat the jerks first, address the neurological / psychiatric side of things rather than going straight for a mechanical fix. I've felt that if at all possible, we would need to involve her in the decision about whether to operate, but now she is so dopey from the anti-jerk medicine that we'll have to get her off that before she can engage with us at all. The plan is now for her to leave hospital and be cared for by nurse-aides, and that we'll wait for her to resurface (I hope she does . . .) or for the hip to pop out again before thinking of an operation.

Trying to respond to the scarily clinical and meaty world of doctors and hospitals, I've thought quite often about the rather different "beads and feathers" approach in "The Blue Sky." Also, I've really been feeling, again, for you and Carole. Apart from the things you mentioned, what is hard for me now is learning to relax in the midst of a state of unknowing to which the habitual response is restless anxiety—is she about to die? Will she need constant care? What do I need to do? etc. This is how you must have been living for some time. So, again, my warmest wishes to you both.

While you are collecting firewood for winter, here it's spring.

With love,

Julia

October 17, 2005

Subject: Re: from Julia: how are things?

Julia, Michael,

Things are OK. As they can be. Carole almost laughs saying, people who weren't expecting to die are dying all the time, all around us (like Tom Killion's wife's niece Jadjee who just died at eighteen of cystic fibrosis), and here am I, expected to die for several years now, just living on.

So we live with a very heightened sense of things. Julia, thanks for the paper on your visit to America/ka. That's precise. May I send it around by email to a few friends?

(Monday the 17th is full moon, and is Autumn Moon Festival time in East Asia. Get some mooncake cookies at a Chinese grocery or restaurant and eat one while looking at the moon—) but I wonder, is this happening in the southern hemisphere? Hmm.

WARMLY,

Gary

> *Recalling the Past at T'ung Pass*
>
> Bunched together   peaks of the ranges
> Raging,   the waves on the banks.
> Snaking along through   mountains & rivers
> The road to T'ung Pass.

I look west, hesitate—and grieve,
Here where armies   once passed through
Palaces of rulers   now but dust.
Empires rise   the people suffer,
Empires fall they suffer again.

—anon

October 17, 2005

Subject: branch, skull, crystal, moon

Dear Gary,

I'd be pleased for you to send the paper around to a couple of friends, but I think you should ask them not to circulate it further. It's due to be published in a journal called *Safundi*, fairly soon I hope. If anyone comments on what I've said, I'd be interested to know. Am not sure how well the narrative essay approach works for this kind of thing.

Thanks for your reminder about the full moon tonight. We have been so caught up in my mother's state of being (back in hospital again yesterday looking very, very ill with suspected kidney failure) that we hadn't really remembered to look up. Still, our boy Sky seems to have been in touch. Last night he dreamt that he was standing on a branch of a tree near the sea when a woman came and chopped the branch. He fell and died, and his body immediately went underground. In a few minutes he was able to find his own skull, which had been changed into a white crystal. The same happened to the other boys. Then they saw the moon, a beautiful pink moon over the sea, and the woman who was now their mother travelled over the sea (in a car!) to reach the moon. [. . .]

So I'll find some moon cakes! Wasn't it Autumn Moon Festival when we met in Taiwan?

Love to all,

Julia

June 8, 2006
Subject: Joy of starlight

My dearest Gary,

It's evening here now and I've been watching the stars and the moon in a clear sky and listening to the waves on the beach half a mile away, and thinking about you and Carole.

The Tara mantra comes to mind—OM TARE TUTARE TURE SVAHA, these syllables over and over, and also this:

> Waves recede.
> Not even the wind ties up
> A small abandoned boat.

The moon is clear
mark of midnight.

I have been trying to call to see how you are, but the phone didn't sound right, and now I understand from David Robertson that you've closed it down for a while. So the children and I sent you both golden light at their bedtime—our kind of *tonglen* practice—and you are much in my thoughts. Michael sends his love.

We are well, but since October last year, things have been hard here with my mother after her hip began dislocating again and again and her mind began wandering into confusions and desperate sadnesses. Witnessing this dissolution is so painful. But it is showing me that neither she nor I nor anyone else can "hold it all together"—and this teaching is liberating. I've been reading and enjoying Pema Chodron's book *The Places That Scare You*, and also remembering from you the insight that "Wilderness may temporary dwindle, but wildness won't go away," which I always find comforting and return to again and again in different ways.

Gary, I wish I could give you a hug, or that we could simply sit together, or that I could help with what needs to be done. Please accept a virtual rendering of these things.

And may the beautiful mantra of the Mother of Wisdom

and Compassion ripple across the world to you both from night into day, winter into summer: this ineradicable joy of starlight, clear moon shining in the heart, and always the waves receding and returning to the shore.

With much love,

Julia

Dear Carole,

I keep remembering the beautiful Japanese fabric of a dress you were wearing at that conference we attended in Taiwan, and your joy and laughter and clarity, and how when my finger had been crushed in a door you heated up a paper clip to plunge it into the nail and release the pus and the pain. We have been thinking about you so much, and the children and I have been sending you golden light from our hearts.

With much love,

Julia

July 2, 2006
Subject: Carole

Dear Julia,

Carole slipped away at 4pm Thursday the 29th. It was a quiet and gentle departure after two days of silence, sleep, unresponsiveness, mouth closed against food or water.

Kimbles were here Friday afternoon, plus Gen, Kai, and Robin. A few close friends came by Saturday morning. Then she went to the funeral home & next week to cremation. Painful as it is, we all know it was fully time for her to go.

Such a hugely sweet and big-hearted person. We loved each other dearly from beginning to end. Memorial gathering won't be till August.

om.ah.hum.

Gary

And Julia, I did read your letter to Carole. She was charmed and grateful that you remembered. . . .

This is harder than I ever thought it would be. . . .

> Tsuyu no yo wa   tsuyu no yo
>   nagara   sarinagara
> This dewdrop world   is but a
>   dewdrop world   and yet
>   —Kobayashi Issa

Kitkitdizze
north of the South Yuba River
near the headwaters of Blind Shady Creek
in the trees at the high end of a bunchgrass meadow
                  —Gary Snyder

July 3, 2006
Subject: Full of heart

Dear Gary,

Thank you for this tender message. Since receiving it this morning, I have been thinking of you both all day on this our twins' ninth birthday.

My friend, I feel for you much in this tough grief which is so full of heart. Been reading again now the lovely poem "Finding the Space in the Heart" which you put at the end of the endless mountains and rivers.

Resting, walking, breathing in and breathing out . . . may you be at ease. Our prayers and blessings travel across the world—

With my love,

Julia

July 4, 2006

Dear Gary,

One more thing, I'm in the last stages of the book I've been writing for the last three years about prehistoric archaeological sites. It's dedicated as follows:

For Gary Snyder
And all our relations

So there you are.

Love,

Julia

Julia,

Thank you so much. For everything. I look forward to seeing this. . . .

Love,

G

Subject: Thank you

Dear Gary,

Well, thank *you*—living as far apart as we do, yet to be close. . . .

I'll print and bind a copy of my manuscript and put in the post for you. No hurry at all, though, to read or respond. [. . .]

With love, as always,

Julia

2008

Dear Julia,

What an amazing book [*A Millimetre of Dust*]. It came. I just got back from the East Coast, I just started reading it.

Thank you for your very kind dedication. It is really something. My deep thanks and more back to you later—working on this book must have brought you deep pleasure!

Warmly,

Gary

February 2009

Dear Julia,

Thank you so much for sending me the "call for papers" and the invitation to attend. Also the phone call, which came in on my old phone in the barn with almost no volume but I could understand you with my ear right down on it. I'm going to shut that phone off. [. . .]

Sounds like a great conference, and of course a challenging topic that we are all still wrestling with.

I am already promised to some sort of seminar with Fish and Wildlife people down in the lava-lands south of Mono Lake on the east side of the Sierra. This is UC Davis scientists involved, and David Robertson got himself and me into it—I'm trusting David. So I can't do both, even if I wanted to (and if / when I do go to South Africa I'll want to plan enough time there to explore around a bit). First priority now is straightening out the land and estate affairs so that when I'm gone, it will be easy for Kai and Gen to take hold and run it all. Simple as it may look, our place is outrageously marginal (legally) to the usual ways large parcels of land are held in California. Back when we were all young up here, everything was done on a handshake.

I am also interested—always—in what you are thinking and working on. Things in the US are unsettled as you know, probably same is true in South Africa—everywhere in the world right now. The university world seems on hold too—especially in California, which is not only out of money but hugely in debt. The plus is that a whole new set of people are seriously thinking about bioregional / local pathways and appreciating simplicity and sustainability. I'm hoping that a "recovery" will not just mean everyone returning to their old bad habits.

Wishing you and Mike and the children the very best in this new year,

lots of love,

Gary

February 16, 2010

Dear Gary—

Thank you for this confluence of new year, hearts and flowers, and Parinirvana. For us, of course, it's summery, though some leaves are beginning to turn.

A quick question: I'm on sabbatical this year and so have some time to do things. Also some research funds. One thought is to meet up with you somewhere and record a conversation. Does this sound like a possibility? And if so, when and where? It needn't be in the US.

I have an invite from Scott Slovic to go to Reno—not sure if I really want to (I don't seem to have much heart at the moment for institutional ecocriticism), but it could connect up with seeing you.

A different thought, of course, would be for you to visit South Africa. As you know, you have an open invitation.

love,

Julia

Early 2010

Dear Julia,

Sure. This does indeed sound like an idea. You should consider visiting Reno; it has become an important and lively place and is doing what we would have hoped the Nature and Culture Program at Davis would do—but didn't make it. I think Davis is too specialized, career conscious, and competitive for the faculty to want to give time to such a thing. There would have been plenty of students, but it was short of faculty and the administration would not really get behind it.

And I like Scott and his wife. And it is only two and a half hours from there to here. And there is a lot of great country accessible from the Reno area, including my favorite desert, the Black Rock.

But if you only had a week or two you could just come here, or meet me anywhere along the line—at the moment, one might think of Tucson, Arizona, in October. But I'm going to put my whole calendar for 2010 in here for reference (see the attachment).

I won't be going overseas much until I get the legalities of land straightened out here so that my sons won't have some later troubles.

Hope all's well with you guys,

best,

Gary

>>>>>

"A painting in a museum hears more ridiculous opinions than anything else in the world."—Edmond de Goncourt (Bob G)

October 16, 2010

Julia,

It was lovely having you here. And I found that I did indeed have that 2005 interview, and in fully edited and revised form, so sent that to Whalen-Bridge, who sent it to Storhoff. And sent along a revised permission form too. You may already have received the electronic copy of that.

It's a lovely and very useful discussion that you provoke there—about *Peaks*—again reminding me how fine a critic & scholar you have been in regard to my work. I had tucked it away, and it had partially slipped from my mind, which made me think they were speaking of this very recent recording we did. Obviously you wouldn't have had time to transcribe it—even if you wanted to.

So relax and be home now, and move into summer even as we are looking ahead to winter. It's overcast today, cool, with showers of rain. For the moment, the fire season is over, though we don't know if it will dry out one more time or not—

Warmly,

Gary

October 19, 2010

Dear Gary—

[. . .] Once again, thank you for the special days I spent with you and Emi. Washing dishes and singing "Twa Corbies," meeting Gen who arrived holding that beautiful tomato, looking at the ecosystems map of California, eating McIntosh apples with granola for breakfast, waking in the tatami room to the light coming in through the beams of the roof, a story of Emi barking at a mother bear and three cubs up a tree, taking off shoes and putting on shoes, at mealtime Emi standing on her hind legs to lick your face and then mine, the grace you said at our supper with Scott and Suzie, the huge blasts of lightning in the night and you padding around turning things off, a house packed with tools and books and quilts and shrines and stories, the sound of the bell in the Poems on the Underground pinned up in my room. In the ponderosa pines, the sound of the shimmering bell through all. And in all this time, talking, talking, and just being together. Lively and comfortable. Thank you, my dear friend.

And yes, it is warm here now. Spring. Did that copy of my book arrive? I sent it from Reno.

With love and a warm hug. A kiss for Emi too.

Julia

January 18, 2011
Subject: October conversation

Dear Gary—

Well, the children have started school today—first day back after the summer break, and first day of high school (our academic year begins in January)—so I too am getting back to work-related things.

This makes me realise that I haven't heard a response from you to the edited text of the conversation we recorded in October, and wonder whether it somehow slipped away. Should I send it again?

I hope you and Emi are well. It's beautifully summery here—long days, and the garden full of birds.

Love,

Julia

January 19, 2011

Subject: Re: October conversation

Dear Julia,

I do have that mail from you with the text of the interview. Thanks for reminding me. It's even in the proper folder, Get Done Now—though some items in the folder go back to September. So it's good you asked me. I found it and will respond in a few days when I get the firewood moved around and one of the generators fixed.

School begins. Sounds like *The Book of Changes*. I wish you all well, and you can hope that your country never becomes a superpower because that's a huge drag.

Warmly,

Gary

Ravens in the afternoon control burn
   smoky haze
croaking away.
Coyotes yipping in the starry early
   dawn.

January 19, 2011

Thanks, my friend.

Yes, things do feel a bit like *The Book of Changes* around here. Yesterday afternoon my mother's blood pressure zoomed up dangerously high and she couldn't stop shaking, but when the children and I went to visit she was witty and cheerful, looking well.

Sorry about the superpower on your side of the planet. You should come and visit over here.

love,

J

February 10, 2011

Dear Julia,

Here's what I've done with the interview. It didn't take much. Feel free to work with it as you choose. I think it's really challenging and fun—basically thanks to you and your charming persistence.

yrz, Gary

Certain religious beliefs, if you have them, are very helpful; but if you do not have them, you can also survive quite happily. Compassion, love, and forgiveness, however, are not luxuries. They are fundamental for our survival.

—Tenzin Gyatso, The Dalai Lama

CREDITS AND ACKNOWLEDGMENTS

I would like to thank Michael Cope for being there right from the beginning, and Barbara Ras at Trinity University Press for her enthusiasm and sensitivity. Thanks as well to the Special Collections staff at the University of California, Davis.

—Julia Martin

"Coyote-Mind: An Interview with Gary Snyder," *TriQuarterly* 79 (Fall 1990), 148–72.

Postcard, March 10, 1992, Box II, 116:53; letter, July 5, 1993, Box II, 116:54; postcard, September 2002, Box II, 219:14, Gary Snyder Archive, Special Collections, University of California, Davis.

"The Present Moment Happening: A Conversation with Gary Snyder about *Danger on Peaks*," *scrutiny2* 12, no. 1 (2007): 157–62.

Gary Snyder and Julia Martin, 1988.

GARY SNYDER is a poet, essayist, and environmental activist. He is the author of eighteen books, among them *Danger on Peaks; Mountains and Rivers Without End; No Nature*, a finalist for the 1993 National Book Award; *The Practice of the Wild; Left Out in the Rain: New Poems, 1947–1985; Axe Handles*, winner of an American Book Award; and *Turtle Island*, which received the Pulitzer Prize for poetry. His honors include the Wallace Stevens Award from the Academy of American Poets, an American Academy of Arts and Letters award, the Bollingen Prize, the John Hay Award for Nature Writing, a Guggenheim Foundation fellowship, the Bess Hokin Prize and the Levinson Prize from *Poetry,* the *Los Angeles Times* Robert Kirsch Lifetime

Achievement Award, the Ruth Lilly Poetry Prize, and the Shelley Memorial Award. He was elected a chancellor of the Academy of American Poets in 2003. He is a professor emeritus of English at the University of California, Davis.

JULIA MARTIN is a South African writer and literary scholar. Her long-standing involvement in the work of Gary Snyder is part of a broader interest in ecological thought, metaphors of interconnectedness, and the representation of place. In addition to her academic work in ecocriticism, she writes creative nonfiction. Her travel memoir, *A Millimetre of Dust: Visiting Ancestral Sites* (2008), is an extended narrative essay about archaeology and the apprehension of deep time. She lives with her family in Cape Town, where she teaches English at the University of the Western Cape.

CPSIA information can be obtained
at www.ICGtesting.com
Printed in the USA
JSHW042034010321
12171JS00001B/1